MW00999650

Protect Your Great Ideas for Free!

Advance Praise

"Without the advice provided by Nevin as set forth in his book, our company would never have survived and would cease to be profitable! Nevin tells you what to do to protect your great idea and how to do it in a way anyone can understand. I guarantee you will learn something when you read his book and have a good time while you are at it!"

—Brad Armstrong, J.D., Recipient of many awards including, Entrepreneur of the Year® sponsored by Ernst & Young, Merrill Lynch, and *Inc.* magazine.

"Nevin has been giving great advice to our students for years. The information found in Nevin's fast-paced, detailed, and funny book arms our graduate students with countless critical questions for the new businesses they start or join about how the businesses have protected their great ideas."

—Gary M. Cadenhead, Ph.D., Director of the MOOT CORP Program and a Senior Lecturer in Entrepreneurship at the McCombs School of Business at the University of Texas at Austin.

"Having difficulty finding a patent/intellectual property attorney who speaks English? Nevin's your man. Using examples of intellectual property that everyone knows and recognizes, Nevin lays out this complex area with spirit and fun and without the typical lawyer gibberish. Nevin's book will give you all the information you need to protect your great idea; just don't get him started on the glory days of Navy football."

—Dr. Ray Smilor, President, Foundation for Enterprise Development, La Jolla, California.

Other Titles of Interest From Maximum Press

Other Top e-business Books

- *101 Ways to Promote Your Web Site*

- *3G Marketing on the Internet*

- *101 Internet Businesses You Can Start From Home*

- and many more...

For more information go to *www.maxpress.com*
or e-mail us at *moreinfo@maxpress.com*

Protect Your Great Ideas for Free!

Free Steps for Protecting the Valuable Ideas Generated by Every Business Owner, Entreprenuer, Inventor, Author, and Artist

J. Nevin Shaffer, Jr., Esq.

Your Plain-Speaking Attorney

MAXIMUM PRESS
605 Silverthorn Road
Gulf Breeze, FL 32561
(850) 934-0819
www.maxpress.com

Publisher: Jim Hoskins

Manager of Finance/Administration: Joyce Reedy

Production Manager: Gina Cooke

Cover Designer: Lauren Smith

Copyeditor: Ellen Falk

Proofreader: Jacquie Wallace

Indexer: Susan Olason

Printer: Malloy, Inc.

Library of Congress Cataloging-in-Publication Data

Shaffer, Nevin, 1948-
Protect your great ideas for free! : (free steps for protecting the valuable ideas generated by every business owner, inventor, author, and artist) / Nevin Shaffer, Jr.
p. cm.
ISBN 1-931644-47-0
1. Intellectual property—United States—Popular works. I. Title.
KF2980.S53 2006
346.7304'8—dc22
2006019082

This book, which is my very first and probably my last, is dedicated to Norma, Ellen and Nevie Shaffer!

Disclaimer

The protection of your great idea is an important and sometimes costly business decision. While the author and publisher of this book have made reasonable efforts to ensure the accuracy and timeliness of the information contained herein, the author and publisher assume no liability with respect to loss or damage caused or alleged to be caused by reliance on any information contained herein and disclaim any and all warranties, expressed or implied, as to the accuracy or reliability of said information.

This book is not intended to replace competent legal counsel in determining the steps to take to protect an idea.

Trademarks

The words contained in this text which are believed to be trademarked, service marked, or otherwise to hold proprietary rights have generally been designated as such by use of initial capitalization. No attempt has been made to designate as trademarked or service marked any words or terms in which proprietary rights might exist. Inclusion, exclusion, or definition of a word or term is not intended to affect, or to express judgment upon, the validity of legal status of any proprietary right which may be claimed for a specific word or term.

Your "Members Only" Web Site

The world changes every day. That's why there is a companion Web site associated with this book. On this site you will find updates to the book and other resources of interest.

To get into the "Members Only" section, go to the Maximum Press Web site located at *www.maxpress.com* and follow the links to the companion Web site for *Protect Your Great Ideas for Free* section. When you try to enter, you will be asked for a password. Type in the following password:

pier

You will then be granted full access to the "Members Only" area. Visit the site often and enjoy the updates and resources with our compliments—and thanks again for buying the book. We ask that you not share the password for this site with anyone else.

Preface

This material is provided for general informational purposes only and should *not* be considered a legal opinion or relied upon in lieu of specific legal advice. Accordingly, readers who require legal services in connection with their specific circumstances should consult an attorney competent in the field of intellectual property. You have been warned!

About This Book

This book is about how to legally protect your great idea for free. It is an "intellectual property law" primer in plain English. If you are in business, if you invent things, or if you are an artist or an author, trust me, you have "intellectual property." Intellectual property law is important because it is the tool you can use to protect your great idea. Once your great idea is protected, at least to a minimum degree, you have the leverage you need to try to make money from your great idea and to resolve the inevitable conflicts that arise with any successful great idea quickly, inexpensively, and in your favor! The first steps you must take to protect your invention, work of art/authorship, brand, or hard-earned "trick of the trade" are not complicated and cost you nothing, but you must take them or you risk losing your great idea forever!

—J. Nevin Shaffer, Jr., Esq.
Your Plain-Speaking Attorney

Table of Contents

Chapter 3:
Free Protection for Your Great Invention   36

Chapter 4:
Free Protection for Your Great Creative Work   64

Chapter 5:
Now Build Your Idea into Something Valuable   75

Chapter 6:
What If I Am an Employee with a Great Idea?   86

Chapter 7:
Meet Jim H (a Hypothetical Guy with a Great Idea and No Money)   89

Chapter 8:
Questions I Hear and You Should Ask   94

Chapter 9:
Final Thoughts   100

Introduction

A great idea is not funny. It is as serious as a heart attack to the person who came up with it! Still, an awful lot of arcane jargon is usually employed to describe how to protect your idea, and believe me, you would rather have a root canal without gas than have to wade through the normal intellectual property information to find out what to do! So understand as we get started that this book is intended to be informative and fun. If you want to become a patent attorney or practice intellectual property law, go to law school! This book is for those who want simple instructions for complex procedures with as little legal jargon as possible! And just because I kid around here and there does not mean that I don't know how important your great idea is to you!

The Importance of Leverage

Standing there in my underwear watching the rockets arch across the sky in my general direction made me very aware of the need for leverage. The Viet Cong had fired the rockets not at us, my seasoned captain assured me, but at the fuel pier somewhat farther up the Mekong River, upon which our patrol gunboat was trapped. We were held tight against the pier where we were docked by the mighty force of that rushing river, and nothing we could do at that moment was going to get us free. So we just watched and waited. Eventually the "attack" ended and I returned to my stateroom to put on some clothes. So ended my first day in Vietnam.

When clients ask me what good intellectual property protection is, I tell them it is powerful leverage, powerful enough to resist being pinned against a pier while their competitors take shots at them! This book will help you understand what types of intellectual property your great idea represents and how to use intellectual property law to protect your great idea. My objective is to give you the information necessary for you to decide what amount of leverage is best for you and what steps you must take to ensure you do not lose your great idea to a competitor. My hope is that when it comes time to fight for your great idea's life, you will have all the leverage you need to make the other guy surrender! And oh yes, you will learn how you can start protecting your great idea for free!

Where Have All the Patent Attorneys Gone?

I sat alone in a humongous room in a federal building in San Antonio, Texas, taking the patent bar exam while the bored imperial proctor looked down on me from a metal desk high above. The good news was that, unlike the dental aptitude test, there was no chalk to carve, and the better news was that I passed the exam on the first try!

I have been a practicing patent attorney since 1980. A "patent attorney" is an attorney licensed in a state and also by the federal government. My bachelor of science degree from the Naval Academy qualified me to take the patent bar exam. Every patent attorney has some sort of technical degree. (The next time you meet a patent attorney, you can wow him or her by asking, "What technical degree do you have?")

Anyway, we used to just call ourselves "patent attorneys," but then someone had the idea that that didn't sound too cool, so why don't we call ourselves "intellectual property" lawyers? Now, I really like that because even though I am not too intellectual (as you can tell from reading just this far), it sure sounds neat and I think it helps get the clients in the door! Also, in addition to sounding highfalutin (as they used to say in the old days), I think it does help folks know that we do more than just patent work. The field of intellectual property law includes the three other major means by which individuals and businesses with great ideas can protect them from their competitors. Not every person or business has a patent, but if you get to the point where you are marketing your great idea, you will have trademarks, copyrights, and trade secrets. This book looks at all four of these basic forms of intellectual property, one at a time, and tells you what steps you must take to prevent your competitors from taking your great ideas!

1

But I Don't Have Any Great Ideas Worth Protecting—Or Do I?

In this chapter you will discover that pretty much every living person, and some dead ones, have protectable ideas! People in business, inventors, software developers—all of these people have ideas, some of them great! Don't be surprised if you see yourself in most, if not all, of the types of idea generators discussed in this chapter.

Everyone Has Ideas...Period!

Are you in business? Have you ever made something to solve a problem because you couldn't find it at WAL-MART? Have you ever written a poem or drawn a picture? If you answered yes to any of these questions, you have ideas. Your ideas are the gold from your mind, your "intellectual property." Unless you are a total slug and have never done anything in your entire life, you have intellectual property. Everyone does! And chances are, some (perhaps a great deal) of your intellectual property is well worth protecting—even if you don't realize it yet (and many don't until it's too late). It's a shame that more people don't realize how easy and inexpensive it is to protect their great ideas. What you will learn in this book is what kind of intellectual property your great idea represents and the steps you can take to protect your great idea for free!

Why Should You Protect Your Ideas Anyway?

What is the point in protecting your great idea? The simple answer is that your ideas are what make you money and/or keep you in business! The more you protect your ideas, the longer you can stay in business; and the longer you stay in business, the more valuable your ideas become! I have heard it said that we are now in the "information age," and in this "high-tech," Internet-connected age what is important are ideas! It's no longer "bricks and mortar" buildings that are important but rather the new ideas a business has, and must have, to stay in business in today's twenty-first-century global market! Well, excuse me if I pour a little water on that campfire. In my opinion, no matter what the century, *it has always been the person or business with the new idea that has set the pace!* How would you like to have cornered the market on that "wheel" invention way back when? Anyway, then and now, ideas rule. Because that is true, a prudent plan for people with ideas includes taking steps to protect a new idea as soon as possible. How sad would it be if you lost your great idea because you didn't know how to protect it from day one? Trust me: it is a sad thing to see. I have had to give many clients over the years the bad news about how they had lost their idea to the public because of the things they did before they came to me. The even sadder part is that they could have protected their idea for free, if they had only known how.

I was going to war. Really. I was the engineering officer on the USS Gallup (Figure 1.1), and as we steamed out of port in Guam on the first leg of the long trip to Vietnam, I had the "conn." In navy talk, this means I was the officer in charge of where the ship went. The captain had gone below, and I was in charge of the lead ship in a group of three. The Gallup set the course and the others followed. It was my first trip to Vietnam on a gunboat and we had a long way to go, but already I was nervous. *I am going to WAR* is what kept going around in my mind. Anyway, all of a sudden I was pitched forward against the window glass as the Gallup came to a screeching stop—or at least as close to a screeching stop as you can get with a ship. Being the new guy, my first thought was "Uh oh! What did I touch?" I looked around the bridge. No one said anything, and no one had a clue what had happened. In the meantime, the other two ships sailed on by, leaving us wallowing in their combined wake, their crews waving happily in response to our misfortune, whatever it was. Well, the captain called the bridge and asked in a very rude manner what was going on. I said I didn't know. That didn't help things much, and he suggested quite rudely that I, as engineering officer, inquire about why "his" ship had stopped moving. So I called the engine room and asked rudely (think stuff flowing downhill)

Figure 1.1. The USS Gallup (PG 85).

why we had stopped. There was a short pause, and then they said, "Doc caught a fish!" Doc was Frank Martin Ivey (Dr. Ivey—What a great name for a doctor!), the squadron medical officer and an avid fisherman. While I was fretting about going to war, he had set up his lawn chair on the fantail and gone fishing! He caught a dolphin (the fish kind), and then yelled down the hatch to the engine room, "Stop the boat! I caught a fish!" and they did! When I told him what had happened, the captain said, "Oh, well, when he gets it in, catch up to the other guys." And I thought, now that's power! That's leverage! No one in the Navy ever messed with the medical officers; likewise, no one will mess with your great idea once you have done what I advise! You will have "legal leverage" after you have protected your great idea for free. Let's start by looking at where these ideas come from.

The Overlooked Protectable Ideas in Every Business

The president of a Pensacola business group asked me what I did, and I told him I was in the protection business. "What kind of protection do you provide for businesses?" he asked. I said, "I help businesses identify and protect their intellectual property—you know, patents, trademarks, copyrights, and trade secrets." "Oh," he said. "We don't have any of that here."

The fact is, if you are in business—even in sunny, scenic Pensacola, Florida (the paradise of the universe, as far as I am concerned!)—you *do* have intellectual property, even if you think you don't. For example, if you sell anything—goods or services—you call the things or the services you sell *something*, don't you? Well, the words, symbols, and slogans you use to identify and distinguish your things from all the other similar things being sold are your **trademarks**. And, surprise, your great ideas for your trademarks are valuable intellectual property! Figure 1.2 shows one familiar example of a trademark, the APPLE Computer logo.

Or have you ever had a great idea for an ad and created an original ad for the thing you are selling? Well, guess what. Original works of authorship, i.e., advertisements, software, and such, are protected by **copyrights,** and copyrights are also valuable intellectual property! Figure 1.3 shows an example of copyrighted software, offered by the MICROSOFT Company on its Web site.

Or does your business have a list of customers or material providers or assembly tricks or great pricing strategies that only you and your employees know about? Watch out! These "secrets" may not be rocket science, but they are **trade secrets,** and (can you guess?) trade secrets constitute even more valuable intellectual property that you or your business own! Figure 1.4 illustrates two of the most famous owners of trade secrets (ingredients, in this case): COCA-COLA and KFC.

The take-home point here is, again, if you are in business, your great business ideas are valuable intellectual property. You may have overlooked your

Figure 1.2. The APPLE Computer logo.

Figure 1.3. The MICROSOFT Web site offers copyright protected software.

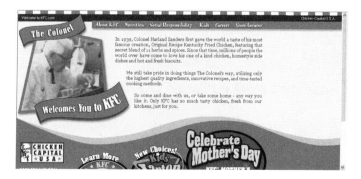

Figure 1.4. COCA-COLA and KFC are examples of companies with trade secrets.

intellectual property up until now because you didn't know you had it. Now that you know your great ideas are valuable intellectual property, however, you will learn in Chapter 2 how to protect your business ideas so that you don't lose them.

Inventors Have Protectable Ideas Too!

"Turn it off, Jack, the pig's turning blue!" These are the immortal words spoken to Jack Cover, inventor of the Taser nonlethal weapon, also called a "stun gun," during an early test of his patented invention. The rest is history!

Not every inventor has a business, and not every business has inventors. Nonetheless, if you have ever faced a problem, were unable to solve it with the resources readily available to you, and then had an idea as to how to solve it yourself, you are an inventor! Even if you just put together part A from RADIO SHACK and part B from TOYS-R-US, it is still an invention and you are an inventor. So now what? Well, if your great idea for an invention is useful and new, and not just an improvement that anyone could have done to solve the problem, then your great idea is protectable by a **patent**!

A patented invention is very powerful intellectual property in its own right, but inventors also have other intellectual property. Thomas Edison kept all of his failed light bulbs because he said they represented a thousand great ideas he knew for sure would not work. Kept confidential, an inventor's failures are trade secrets that may be worth more than the final invention! Obviously, many businesses have been founded on patentable great ideas, but inventors have lots of intellectual property even without having patents.

Knowing you are an inventor is the first step! Knowing what to do to protect your great idea is the next! You will learn what inventors must do to protect their great ideas in Chapter 3.

What About Authors and Artists? Do They Have Protectable Ideas?

My son's fourth-grade class wrote a book about Hurricane Ivan. Each student contributed to the short story and drew a picture about the hurricane. The book, *When the Hurricane Blew* (see Figure 1.5), is now available at BARNES & NOBLES and AMAZON.com, and my son, Nevie, has met the governor of Florida and had several book signings! The book is a big success! Since he was

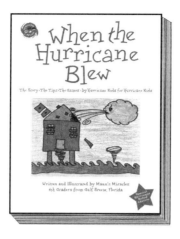

Figure 1.5. The book, *When the Hurricane Blew.*

little, I have told Nevie that every original work of art and authorship that he creates is protectable by copyright, but I never thought he would beat me to the market with a book of his own!

Here is the point. It does not matter how old or young you are; if you have a great idea and create an original work of art or write an original software program, story, poem, song, movie, or ad, you have created valuable copyright intellectual property. You are an artist, an author, and an intellectual property owner! The question is, will you take steps to protect your great idea or not? You will learn what authors and artists must do to protect their great ideas in Chapter 4.

Ignorance Is Not Bliss!

It's hot in any engine room, but it is really hot in the engine room of a ship sailing during the summer in the South China Sea. I know because I was there as the engineering officer on that patrol gunboat I mentioned earlier. The good news was that as we patrolled the Vietnamese coast, we were always running over stuff—fishing nets, lines, and things. It was good news because it gave me an excuse to tell the captain, "Strange noise in the reduction gear. I'd better check it out!" Most of the time the captain would say OK, and two of us would get to scuba-dive around for a half an hour or so, pulling stuff off and banging on the bottom of the boat and generally having a good time, while everyone else sweated it out topside. There was usually plenty of sea life swimming with us too, including these cute little sea snakes. Now I knew that snakes were more afraid of me than I was of them, and I never gave them a thought until one day we exchanged magazines with another ship. The *National Geographic* article I read explained that the sea snakes common to the South China Sea were the deadliest snakes in the world, and the only reason people weren't killed all the time was because they have little mouths! Well, that ended my goofing off in a hurry because I knew it would be just my luck to run into some big-mouthed snake! After that I let the navy divers clean the bottom whenever we got into port, no matter how much stuff we were dragging around!

Here's the point: Ignorance is *not* bliss, because you could die from it! If you read this book, you will learn what kinds of little things can kill your great idea. You will also learn how to protect your great idea for free, and once you have taken the steps to protect your great idea, something neat happens. You have even more options on how to maximize the value of your great idea and how to end threats to your idea. Your idea won't die—it will thrive!

2

Free Protection for Your Great Business Ideas

Business is where it's at in the United States. It's what we do, and it's the reason a discussion of business ideas is the primary focus of this book. In this chapter you will come to understand that virtually every business is an idea-generating machine and that there are many overlapping ways to protect the great ideas that come out of every successful business, some of which can be done for free!

Every Business Has Ideas—Are They Protected?

You should read this if you are a small, medium, or large business owner and have not memorized your intellectual property lawyer's phone number. If you thought intellectual property was only for rocket scientists or computer nerds, this chapter is for you. If you were too busy building your business to pay attention to the details of protecting your great business ideas, read on! This chapter will review the intellectual property assets every business has and explain how to evaluate them and what to do to protect them from your competitors. Finally, as the title of the book suggests, each idea that you choose to protect can and should be protected for free, at least to start with. Learn how now!

What Is a Brand, and Why Should You Care?

Whatever business you are in, you call yourself something and you sell something, either goods or services. Typically, the company name reflects the product sold. The COCA-COLA Company owns the trademark COCA-COLA, for example. This simplifies things, I suppose, but it is not a requirement for doing business. Many company names have nothing to do with the thing they are selling. Procter & Gamble sells no "Procter" this or "Gamble" that, but they have lots and lots of words, symbols, and slogans they do use as their marks of trade. Remember, the people you are trying to sell to use trademarks to help them identify and distinguish competing products and services by price, quality, origin, and source. Therefore, for the people who buy from you, the trademarks, or brands, your business adopts become the repository of all the data about your product or service in a single word, symbol, or slogan. That sounds important. Is it?

A Shortcut to Other People's Money

When our daughter, Ellen, was very young, not more than two or three years old, I had her strapped in a bucket in the back seat of my car while driving around Austin, Texas. I was fantasizing how much fun it would be when she grew up and I started buying her prom dresses and giving her an allowance and stuff. (Hey, don't ask me why I would fantasize about that! I was a demented new dad!) Anyway, all of a sudden out of the back seat comes this little voice screaming, "Fries! Fries! Fries!" Can you guess what hallowed symbol of American commerce she had seen? That is correct—the golden arches themselves! Now think about that for a second. I had, essentially, an alien life-form strapped in the back seat of my car that could not read, write, or speak very much English, and she was telling me how to spend my money! Now that is powerful stuff. Don't you want something like that? The truth is, behind trademark attorneys' authentic lawyer gibberish, trademarks are the shortcuts people use to give you their money. They are the shortcuts you use to give other people your money. When you want a DIET COKE, you do not read the label; you do not even read the words. You take the silver can with the red stripe and put the 50 cents on the counter and you are out the door. You are a busy businessman/woman with great ideas!

A shortcut that people use to give you their money. A shortcut to other people's money. A shortcut to money! Now that sounds like you're on to something, doesn't it?

What Is the Value of a Brand?

Assuming you agree with me that a shortcut to other people's money sounds like a good thing, you might be surprised to learn that brands also have a value of their own! It's true. Let's suppose "money is no object" (words, by the way, you should never say to a lawyer) and you wanted to buy the COCA-COLA Company. Well, you would have to write a check for around $70 billion dollars for the capital equipment, buildings, and such. But if you also wanted the two words COCA-COLA, you would have to write a second check for about $102 billion dollars! But, hey, money is no object, right? The point is that, in this case, the brand is more valuable than the company itself. How cool is that!

Now, your brand is not worth anything near that; few are. But every brand has some value. How much did you spend on advertising last year? What is the difference between the capital assets of your business and what it would sell for? That value is the "goodwill" of your business, and guess what a brand does? A brand represents the goodwill of a company—yours, Coke's, and anyone else's. Now, some companies have no goodwill because either bad things have happened (ENRON comes to mind) or they are brand new. But if you have a good product or service and you stay in business, your brand will gain value over time, all the time. Wouldn't it be great, then, if you could get a brand that lasted forever? Well you can!

What Is the Value of a Registered Brand?

A registered trademark or brand is an application for the registration of a mark that has been examined on the state or federal level, or both, and allowed to register. The advantage of a state registration is that in many states, registering the mark protects you in all parts of the state, even if you have only one store! Likewise, a federal registration protects your mark in all 50 states, territories, and possessions of the United States. Once a mark is registered, government agents work tirelessly on your behalf rejecting applications for marks that are the same as, or similar to, your registered mark for the same or similar goods or services. It is truly the last great government service in the country! And it gets better! A trademark registration may be renewed every 10 years and thus last forever! Think about it: The world will have to end for NIKE Inc. to lose the rights to the word NIKE! Now that is a very strong asset for any company: a shortcut to other people's money that lasts forever!

What Types of Brands Are Registrable?

So the good news is, registered marks last forever! The bad news? Not every word, symbol, or slogan you may pick is registrable! While it is true that you can pick any word, symbol, or slogan you want ("it's a free country" after all), not every one you pick will pass the test for registration.

The first thing you need to understand when picking a brand is that you are playing a game and you do not yet know all the rules. I don't know about you, but I have never done too well playing games when I didn't know the rules. I quit playing make-up games with our son when he was little for just that reason. I would think I had won and he would explain that, no, I hadn't, because of a rule I didn't know about!

The First Rule

The first rule to learn about picking a brand is that you cannot register a mark that has already been registered. So the first step in picking a mark that is registrable is to make sure you haven't picked one that is already registered. Sounds simple enough, but you need a bit more data.

The United States Patent and Trademark Office organizes all the goods and services on the planet into 45 classifications; classes 1–34 are for goods and classes 35–45 are for services. (Just 45? If I were the king of Trademark world, I think I would go for at least a hundred classes or so.) Anyway, every mark is placed in one or more of these classes depending on what is being sold. Usually, when you are selling one product it will be registered in one class. One registration, however, does not cover products in other classes. Old Goat computers would be registered in International Class (IC) 9, for electronic goods, but this class would not cover Old Goat T-shirts, which would be sold in IC 25, for clothing. So remember, everything goes in one of the 45 classes.

The next thing you need to know is that it is OK to have the exact same mark registered for two different things so long as there is "no likelihood of confusion in the innocent consumer's mind" as to the origin and source of the goods or services. (This subjective analysis is the actual legal test that is applied. More on this later.) So, for example, you will find the mark McDONALD'S registered for both restaurant services and pump parts because no one has ever driven up to the parts store and asked for a BIG MAC. However, if the parts store put up some golden arches and started selling "McWrenches," it would be in big trouble!

The Second Rule

Again, the first basic rule is that if there is already a pending application or registration for the same or a similar mark for the same or a similar thing, start over! The second basic rule is if the mark you have picked is merely descriptive of the thing you are selling, it is *not* registrable! This is the cause of some major forehead furrowing when I am talking with clients who have picked a trademark without knowing the rules (meaning just about everybody I have ever talked to!). It is a simple rule, really, and quite understandable. The government is not going to give any one person the exclusive right until the end of time to the word apple for fruit. If they did, you would have to say, "Want to buy a banana? It's really an apple, but Shaffer, that sneaky trademark lawyer, got his client the right to the word, and I can't use it."

The problem with the second rule, however, is not that it is complicated, but that it runs counter to the way we, meaning real people, use trademarks. People, even trademark attorneys, use brands descriptively, and the non–trademark attorney people in the world therefore assume that a good brand describes the product. Wrong! And where does this mistaken idea come from? It comes from the fact that from the moment we get up until the moment we go to sleep, we are immersed in a sea of advertising, and we sometimes have complete conversations with people in which we say nothing but brand names: "Drove my HONDA to SEARS, picked up a DIEHARD and a pair of NIKES, had a BIG MAC and a COKE." That's the way we talk! That sentence consists of nothing but federally registered brand names, and you understand everything that was said there and a lot about the person who said it. You know the price, quality, origin, source, stock price, etc. of the type of car he drives, shoes he wears, and food he eats! That is a lot of information in a few tiny shortcuts. And that is why when a business picks a brand name for its new blue pen, for example, they think, "'The Blue Pen'! It's perfect! It sings!" Well, it will have to sing because it is not registrable, and anyone else selling blue pens can call them blue pens too.

Not All Registered Marks Are Created Equal

OK, now you know that in order for you to register a brand, the same or a similar brand must not already have been registered for the same or a similar product. Also, you know that you can't register your first choice, the name that describes exactly what you are selling. But here is the most important part. Even if you pick a brand name that passes those two tests, not all registrable marks are created equal! To start with, let me ask you this; Would you prefer a "bad" brand that is hard (think "expensive") to register and hard (think "very expensive") to defend once it is registered, and that gains value slowly over time? Or would you rather have a "good" brand that is easy to register and easy to defend and that gains value quickly? You want a good brand, obviously, unless you don't care, you are a humongous company with tons of cash flow and "money is no object," and you have all the intellectual property lawyers you will ever need and you want to keep them busy. My assumption is that most of you would rather have a good brand! Well, how do you pick one of the good kinds? Read on!

Picking a Brand That Doesn't Stink!

Brad Armstrong, good friend and former law partner of mine, came to me one day and said that he was going to start a moving company. He said his experience with movers in the past had suggested that a particular character trait was commonly missing. The missing trait, he said, was honesty. So he said he had the great idea to call his new company Honest Movers moving company. Since I was his friend, partner, and trademark attorney, he asked me what I thought of the idea for his brand. I told him, "It has an extraordinarily high likelihood of failing at least one of the requirements for registration," or some such polite lawyerly doubletalk. Being a smart lawyer and a very good entrepreneur, he said "Huh?" And I said, "In layman's terms: It stinks!" Once we discussed these matters more fully, he came up with the great idea of Blue Whale Moving Company as his brand. His company has been extraordinarily successful, and the "good" brand he picked is a major key to its success, in addition to that honesty thing!

Character Traits of a Good Brand

Knowing the character traits of good brands will help you pick one. To begin with, the owner of a mark must always use the mark as what it legally is: an adjective. There is no verb "to XEROX," and it is not a noun. The proper use of the brand is "Please make a copy of this on my XEROX brand photocopier." People, however, use trademarks descriptively all the time, as we have discussed. This does *not*, however, make the brand a generically descriptive term. The only way a brand, once registered, becomes descriptive is if the owner uses it descriptively. This is what has happened to previously registered terms such as "aspirin," "linoleum," "dry ice," and "escalator." Now when you go up to the counter and ask for some "aspirin," the attendant will say, "What brand? We have a lot of choices. Would you like BAYER aspirin or EXCEDRIN or what?" This also accounts for the conversation that occurs at drive-throughs where you say, "Give me a COKE" (meaning any cold drink) and the attendant says, "Will PEPSI do?" Because COKE is a specific brand, if you ask for COKE they must give you that brand and not another, or else tell you they don't have it. (When I was much younger and just out of the navy, I heard that the COCA-COLA Company had a deal where they sent people into bars to order a "rum and COKE," and if they gave them rum and something else, they would slap a 30-page legal document on them! I thought, after seven years as a sailor that that was definitely a job I could handle with little or no additional training!)

The First Step in Picking a Good Brand

All right, now you know that a brand is an adjective and must be used as such by the owner. The very first step, then, in picking a good brand must be to make a list of words you think might make a good brand. No, it's not! But that is what most people do! No, the first step in picking a good brand is to write down what it is that you are selling. Think about the most generically descriptive short term that describes your product or service. On your death bed, when they who intend to inherit everything ask you, "What did you sell, Granddad?" you will tell them: cars, shoes, planes, car repair services, clothes, batteries... you get the picture. Do not go with "the most incredibly innovative tennis shoe known to man." Save that for the advertisement. Stick with "shoes." The shorter and more descriptive, the better!

The Second Step in Picking a Good Brand

OK, now for the fun part. Once you have figured out what it is you are selling, pick a word that has absolutely no relationship to it. That's right, no relation, no connection, and no reason to be associated with it. Think: trying to push two north poles of a pair of magnets together. Think, for example, APPLE Computers. This is a genius of a mark! Remember it and keep it always in front of you as the epitome of all marks great and good, the top dog, the head cheese, the big banana...oops. Anyway, look at that brand. Is APPLE good or bad by itself? You can't tell. If the mark was for fruit, forget about it! But because there is no logical, normal, everyday association with the thing being sold, it is solid gold. Why? Well, because before the company applied, there were no other fruit brand computer marks pending or registered. So the trademark examining attorney had only to decide if the mark was descriptive of the product (even non-trademark attorneys can answer that one!), and bingo, it was registered! So, like I said, the first advantage of selecting a "good" mark is that it is easy to register!

(Now for a short aside about traditional trademark attorney mantras, which you can skip in order to avoid corrupting your database. The standard line in trademark law is that made-up words, like XEROX or EXXON, are best because they mean nothing in any language and they too are easy to register. I disagree for reasons set forth fully hereafter. But also, it seems to me like there are a lot of made-up "X"-type words out there already, so I wonder how good they are really? Now back to our regular program.)

Another Advantage in Picking a Good Brand

Another advantage of a "good" brand is that, once registered, a good brand is easy to defend. Now, I am a lawyer; my Uncle Jake went to law school when he was 65, and he is a lawyer to this day; my sister, Floy, is a lawyer; and my best friend, John Albert Sullivan III, is a lawyer. Lawyers are like friends and family to me! But even friends and family begin to stink after three days or so! My point is, you will need lawyers for every commercially successful business you create; you just don't want them moving in with you! You want to give your lawyers the leverage they need to end your conflict quickly, inexpensively, and in your favor! And good brands are great leverage! For example, let's say you are APPLE Computers with your registered mark, and Banana Computers opens up. You know you aren't Banana and they know they aren't Apple, so that's the end of it, right? Wrong. The legal test for trademark issues is "Is there a likelihood of confusion *in the hypothetical innocent consumer's mind* as to the origin and source of the goods?" Because Apple is such an arbitrary and fanciful mark, there is not only a likelihood but a certainty of confusion associated with the use of the Banana name. As a result, all it would take to end this trademark dispute would be an e-mail saying, "Stop or die!" That's it. No expensive depositions. No really expensive "expert" opinions. No drawn-out, really, really expensive courtroom drama. In fact, no attorney bills at all! One free e-mail and it's over! There is a certainty of confusion in the consumer's mind. The consumer couldn't care less, and has no clue, what APPLE's marketing plans are. After all, MACINTOSH is a type of apple. Maybe, the innocent consumer might think, they are branching out into other fruitful areas!

So now that you see the advantage of a good brand, how do you pick a "great" one?

Shaffer's Recipe for Picking a "Great" Brand

What is the height in feet of Mt. Fujiyama? What are the names of the five Great Lakes? Both Ellen and Nevie know! And so will you when you finish reading this section. It has a lot to do with my theory of how to pick a great mark, not just a good one.

It's All About Memory!

Harry Lorayne and Jerry Lucas wrote a wonderful book on how to remember things, called *The Memory Book* (pretty catchy, huh?) (copyright 1974, published by Ballantine Books). Lorayne says everybody has a good memory; we just do not use it! He outlines a tremendous way to "learn" anything by associating the thing you want to know or learn with something you already know. Teachers use this method whenever they can. Can you remember the name of a country because of its shape? Sure! What is the country that is shaped like a boot? Just about everybody knows the answer. Lorayne says that if you make a connection between the word you know ("boot") and the thing you want to know (the name of the country that looks like a boot, "Italy"), you will never forget it. Something silly is best, he says: "*I totally* (sort of sounds like "Italy") love gigantic boots" could be the phrase you use. When you say it and you are thinking country names, boots and Italy will be forever linked.

Try the Lorayne system now and see if you can learn the height of Mt. Fujiyama. Close your eyes and form the picture of a huge calendar instead of a mountain in your mind. You must actually visualize it. Actually see it in your "mind's eye." A calendar so big it is covered with snow at the top. Do you see it? Now, how many months are there in a year? And how many days are there in a regular year? So how tall is Mt. Fujiyama? That's correct, Mt. Fujiyama is 12,365 feet high! Good job! If you formed the picture in your mind, you will never forget that! OK, let's try another one. Now close your eyes and picture five gigantic homes around a lake. I mean humongous HOMES. The five Great Lakes are Huron, Ontario, Michigan, Erie, and Superior. And now your kids can wow your guests like mine do!

Tom "the Professor" Sisson is a great intellectual property lawyer and a better friend, and he and I used this memory system to get through law school. (We not only got through law school, we were the recipients of the rarely awarded Judge Learned Hand prize. See Tom for details.) The point is, Lorayne's memory system made me think about what a great mark does. A good mark associates itself in many ways with the product or service. A great mark, in my opinion, is also fun and memorable, and it works like a splinter in a person's brain so that they will have to die to forget the mark even if they never buy the product or service! (OK, that might be a little too harsh of an image—but you get the idea.) In short, I believe that a great mark causes people to laugh or cry or drop dead every time they hear it, and is impossible to forget!

A Real-Life Example

This all sounds pretty weird to you, perhaps. How about a real-life example? I was driving down the road in Austin one hot Texas day (that is the usual case with days in Texas from my experience) when the news guy said that the fastest-selling doll in America was the CABBAGE PATCH doll. Now, this was before kids for me, so I wasn't thinking of buying one, but I wondered, "Why is it the fastest-selling doll in America? Is it a stinky, leafy thing or what?" Anyway, I went to a party where the host and hostess had children, and they had one. I picked the doll up and turned it around and around, repeating, mantra-like, "CABBAGE PATCH, CABBAGE PATCH, CABBAGE PATCH." Then I threw it down and said, "It's a goofy-looking doll!" To this day, even though I have kids, I have never bought a CABBAGE PATCH brand doll. Still, when I am on my death bed and my daughter asks me, "Dad, before you go, can you name three dolls?" I will answer, "Sure. BARBIE, CABBAGE PATCH, and I don't know!" Now that's a great mark! I never even bought a CABBAGE PATCH doll, and it's one of only two doll brands I can actually name!

So combining memory tricks with trademark law led me to conclude that a great mark is a simple word that is logically represented by an image. Images are good. They help you remember the height of Mt. Fujiyama and the names of the Great Lakes, don't they? If I say to you, "What image comes to mind when I say the word 'elephant'?" What do you see in your mind's eye? A giraffe? A peacock? No, you see a big grey thing with a long trunk and big ears and all that. And the cool thing is, no matter what language you speak, the image is the same for an elephant everywhere on the entire planet!

Want a Great Mark? Think APPLE Computers!

APPLE Computers, in my opinion again, is an example not of a good mark but of a great mark. It really does sing! Plus it is user friendly in other ways. I am no advertiser, and even I can think up an ad for that brand. Let's see: "An APPLE a day keeps you healthy, wealthy, and wise!" "Put an APPLE on every teacher's desk!" Not great, for sure, but something! What can I do with another very well-known computer company brand, IBM? Hmmmm. "Big Blue" doesn't jump off the page at me for some reason, and I am not sure what it means. And what is their image anyway? On the other hand, what image comes to mind when I say the word "Apple?" Not a banana, that's for sure.

No Lost Sales!

And another thing: Because there is an image logically associated with the brand name, you don't lose sales due to the confusion or forgetfulness of the consumer, who, as you know, has plenty of other choices. Imagine you are a total computer novice and someone says to you, "You must buy an APPLE computer." So you go into the computer warehouse and there are thousands of computers for sale of all makes, models, and brands. You have forgotten what the friend told you and you can't even speak English, and the salesperson says, "What do you want, Bub?" So you look around in desperation and suddenly you see a sign hanging down with a picture on it, and you point to it and the salesperson says, "OK," and the sale is done! What image did you see? An Apple! How great is that?

On the other hand, how does this work with other brands? Let's say, for example, that your friend says, "You must buy a COMPAQ computer. And I will even write it down for you so you don't forget!" This time when you go into the warehouse you can speak the language, and you even show the salesperson the note and he says, "Sure, we got those! You know, of course, that HP bought them, don't you?" And you say, "I didn't know and I don't care! Just get me the computer my friend told me to buy." And he says, "OK, but you know, this handwriting is a little hard to read. Are you sure it is a COMPAQ and not Compuad or Computers R Us?" "Hey," you say, "I don't know. I guess it could be any one of those." And he says, "Well, forget about those. My brother Bill puts together the greatest computer known to man." And the sale is lost!

So, Shaffer says, great brands are simple words with an image. They can be anything so long as there is no logical connection between the mark and the product. There are lots of them out there; you just never paid attention. DOMINO'S is what I am talking about as opposed to PIZZA HUT. In the pizza business, is there any way PIZZA HUT can stop a company from naming its brand Pizza this, that, or the other thing? Not easily, that's for sure, and not cheaply either. On the other hand, game-inspired pizza company names are a no-go thanks to DOMINO'S! I like TOMBSTONE too. It may be a little too edgy for some, though. I can hear someone say, "You try a piece first!" I should point out that there are some really memorable, surely unforgettable marks that will never work, like Nazi brand kosher pickles. Forget about it. (Side comment: All this talk of food is making me hungry. How about you?)

To sum up, a great mark translates into a common image known, preferably, in every culture: Sand Dune, Pine Tree, Oak Leaf, Red Dragon, Dolphin! My Pensacola personal favorite is SQUISHED MOSQUITO software. How great is that! I have no idea what kind of software it is and I have never bought any of it, but I will never, ever forget it!

Not Ready for Greatness?

As a trademark attorney during the 1990s "dotcom" daze, I came to understand that there are some businesses that will never buy into the "Apple" type of great mark. Even though the APPLE Computer company was and is into some very sophisticated technology, the dotcom folks would tell me, "Our industry is very sophisticated, and we can't do a silly brand." Or "The industry is so small that everybody knows everybody, and we don't need a great brand." Or "Only the presidents of companies see our product, so we don't need a brand for the masses." My thought was, and still is, that very sophisticated people and presidents and such all have other choices of goods and services. They may very likely have more choices than the rest of us. But my response, once I explained the pros and cons to them, was "Hey, I don't care what you pick! It's your business, not mine, but don't come crying to me when it is rejected as descriptive or because it is similar to another, prior mark or nobody can remember it. After all, I know money is no object to you dotcom guys!" (Or words to that effect.)

The Product or Service Defines the Brand, Not Vice Versa!

The mistake made by folks who reject arbitrary and fanciful brands because they are "silly" is a common one. Many people reject a great mark because they think that if the mark is "silly," people will think the product is silly too. Wrong. The brand *never* defines the product. The product *always* defines the brand. IBM and other sophisticated companies probably gave APPLE Computers millions of dollars of free advertising by laughing about how silly the new brand was. "Ha ha ha! A 'personal' computer! Right! Like one day there will be one of those in everyone's home!" Stuff like that and worse. But that's not the point, is it? No, the point is, if the product actually was silly, that's what the brand would have come to mean. "Yeah, I bought two Apples and gave them to my kids to play with for a few hours until they turned into a pile of goo." But the product was *not* silly, and no one in the business machine community is laughing about the APPLE brand computer now.

In short, it does not matter how silly or serious the brand is; the product defines what the brand means, i.e., the price, quality, origin, and source. I could dress up in a coat and tie (something I rarely do now that I have given up litigation and don't have to go to court anymore!) and hold up my cheap blue pen and say my serious brand very seriously: "Buy STERLING blue pens." Then when I sell one, the consumer looks at it and says to himself, "Oh, STERLING means cheap blue pens." Again, the product defines the brand, and not the other way around.

One Reason to Pick a "Bad" Brand

While we're at it, in the interest of full disclosure, I actually can think of one instance where having a mark that is pretty close to another guy's mark would be a very good thing. Let's say your business plan is to sell really cheesy pizza. I don't mean pizza with lots of cheese; I mean bad pizza. Your plan is to sell as much bad, cheap pizza as you can. That plan screams for you to find a weak, suggestive mark used by a company that sells good pizza so that you can get as close to it as possible! For example, you might consider PIZZA HOME. Because the U.S. Trademark Office has allowed pretty much any brand using Pizza that wasn't identical to a previously registered mark, you probably would have a good shot at getting PIZZA HOME registered. Then what will happen is that busy people can't remember if it is PIZZA HUT or PIZZA HOME that has the "10 percent off" sale on Tuesdays, and they will keep staggering into PIZZA HOME week after week and buying your cheesy pizza! And it is all perfectly legal as far as the U.S. Trademark Office is concerned. Certainly, however, your business plan should include massive funds in reserve for fighting the lawsuit by PIZZA HUT, but hey, money is no object, and you might even win and not go bankrupt! At least you have an argument. Unlike the situation with Banana Computers, when PIZZA HUT sues you, you can say, "No way there is any confusion whatsoever; you're a Hut, for crying out loud! We are a Home. Mom opens the door for all our clients. We have linen tablecloths, etc."

Trademark Quiz to Test Your New Knowledge

OK, for those of you who have read all of this discussion about trademarks, the following quiz to test what you have learned should be a piece of cake. Feel free to skip it if the discussion has left your eyes in danger of becoming permanently crossed.

True or False: You have trademarks.

True. If you are in business, you sell something, either goods or services. The words, symbols, and slogans you use to identify and distinguish what you sell from all other, similar goods or services are your trademarks.

True or False: Incorporating my company name is the same as trademarking my name.

(This is a trick question because I didn't discuss this. Still, I get asked about this all the time.) False. The process of obtaining a corporate name involves selecting a name that is acceptable to the government. That sounds like trademark selection, doesn't it? It is not. You are dealing with a totally different bureaucrat. This bureaucrat's purpose is to make sure the tax bill gets to the right company!

True or False: I can always use my own name as a trademark.

Wrong (and false too). Trademark rights are first come, first served; the first person to obtain a federal registration for a particular name for a particular type of good or service has the right to prevent the same or a confusingly similar name from being used thereafter for the same or similar things. So if your name is McDonald, forget about using it as a brand for your restaurant. If it is Dell, computer businesses are out. Same with Mike for tennis shoes…too close to NIKE.

True or False: A good trademark describes exactly what you are selling.

Still false! Again, we sometimes have complete conversations with people in which our speech consists of nothing but brand names. There is nothing wrong with people using brands descriptively, but a trademark will not be registrable if it is simply descriptive of the thing being sold. Apple for fruit is *not* registrable, while Apple for computers was perfectly registerable.

> ***True or False:*** Brands become descriptive when the public uses them descriptively.

Not true! Because people use brands generically, they often believe the mark must in fact be generic. Nope. If you use "KLEENEX" generically to mean "tissue," that is OK in general conversation. However, if you use it at a drugstore, they must give you KLEENEX brand facial tissues if they have them. The only way a mark becomes generic is if the owner of the mark uses it descriptively. This is what happened to the previously registered brands "aspirin," "linoleum," "dry ice," and "escalator."

> ***True or False:*** A trademark is a shortcut people use to give you their money.

Absolutely true.

> ***True or False:*** A federally registered mark prevents others from using the same or a similar mark for the same or similar things.

True indeed.

> ***True or False:*** A federally registered trademark lasts forever.

Powerfully true! What a country!

Free Steps You Can Take Yourself to Protect Your Brand

When I say "free," I mean no legal fees or lawyers involved whatsoever, and usually no or little cost involved. Because you are going to have to pay expenses with or without a lawyer, the "free" way to protect your idea basically means "lawyer-free."

Just Use It!

As mentioned earlier, trademark rights are "first come, first served." So if you are the first person to have used a particular word, symbol or slogan to identify and distinguish your product or service, all you have to do to get rights to it is use it! It is that simple! You do not need a lawyer! You do not have to pay anybody or file any forms. Even better, it is legal to—and you should—put the letters TM after your product brand and SM after your service brand. There is also no requirement to pay or file anything in order to use those letters legally after your brand. They just mean, in effect, "Excuse me for living. I didn't spend any money on registering it yet, but this is still my mark!"

Note that you can use the symbol ® only after you get, if you ever do, a federal registration. Also, the same ® symbol is used with both registered trademarks and service marks. And another thing, there is no particular symbol, other than TM or SM, that you get to use if you secure a state registration. (I've always thought that a state trademark should have something like CA in a circle for a California registered mark. Will someone bring this to the attention of the governors at their next get-together?)

The "free" rights you receive if you are the first to use a brand with a particular good or service are called "common law rights of first use." These rights are limited in geographic scope, however. You don't get priority in all of New York by opening your Ground Hog dry cleaning operation in Long Island. It takes years of continuous use to get the rights to extend to all of a city, county, and beyond and requires a lot more than one shop. You should be able to more clearly understand the benefits of registration, either state or federal, at this point!

Do Your Own Search!

Another thing you should consider doing, even before using a brand, is a search. You can search state databases and the federal database of pending, registered, and abandoned brands from the comfort of your home or office! (See Appendix A for a step-by-step discussion of the process for both a federal search and a state search.) You can also hire an intellectual property lawyer to do a professional search—but we are talking "free" stuff here, and lawyers aren't free! ("Free the lawyers!") That is, what I meant to say is that lawyers charge for their time. However, if you are a big-time risk taker, you do not even have to spend any energy, much less money, on a search. Of course, that strategy carries a higher risk of getting a nasty letter from a big-time New York City lawyer saying, "Hey, our client owns the right to the brand NIKE for clothing. You have 30 seconds to stop using it for your T-shirts."

Use Your Brand Properly!

The next free thing you can do to protect your mark is to use it properly in your advertising. That means always using it as an adjective and never as a noun or verb, and never making it plural or possessive. (See Appendix A for a sample Trademark Usage Guide.) Remember, if the owner of the mark uses the mark descriptively, it will eventually become descriptive! Also, make the brand the biggest thing on the page and make it always stand out on the page. Not "nike TENNIS SHOES," but "NIKE tennis shoes." You would be surprised how many advertising experts I have met who have advised my clients to use the mark descriptively and in lower case so as not to mess up the "message." My response is, be careful who you take legal advice from! It doesn't cost a thing to do it right, but you can lose the entire mark if you do it wrong.

I know that someone will be inspired by this discussion to pay attention to how trademarks are used. They will look at the can of COKE they are drinking and will say to themselves, "This guy is just wrong! There is not a single word on the entire can that says anything like 'soda' or 'pop.' In fact, COKE is used by itself, and descriptively, and it is still registered. What's up with that?" What's up is that some marks are "famous," and for famous marks like COKE the basic rules do not apply! One of the main ways a mark gets to be famous is by spending billions on advertising for it. A billion-dollar ad campaign definitely has no place in a "free" protection strategy.

Maximum Protection for Your Brand: Time and Cost

First of all, there is no law that says you must hire an intellectual property lawyer to do any of the things required for maximizing your rights to your ideas in any of these areas. You can do any or all of these things yourself. You can also build your own automobile if you like! The point is, if you are serious about obtaining the maximum protections under intellectual property law, it is best to at least consult a licensed intellectual property lawyer, and everybody knows that lawyers charge for their services!

A Federal Trademark Registration

That said, the maximum protection for any brand is a federal registration. The cost for this protection, when amortized over the life of a federal registration—i.e., forever—is nothing. Therefore, the $100,000 fee to secure a federal registration is cheap, right? Sure, even if it really did cost that much! You will be happy to know, however, that the cost to register a mark that is registrable is more like a hundredth of that, including government fees and attorney fees, if you do use an attorney! One strategy for new businesses to consider is to rely on free common law rights of first use until the cash flow picks up, and then spring for a federal registration.

Again, when you are considering adopting a brand, the first thing you should do is search it. Trademark searches are much more inclusive and conclusive than patent searches and can be very inexpensive—in the hundreds, not hundreds of thousands. The money spent on having your brand searched, whatever amount it is, will more than offset the pain and expense of opening for business and finding that you have no rights to the brand on your new expensive sign, which consequently has to come down tonight!

"Intent to Use" or "Use" Based

Once you have searched your proposed brand, you have two options for staking a claim to your brand at the United States Patent and Trademark Office. You can file right away, even before you open for business or use the brand on your product in commerce. This is called an "intent to use" application and is based on your swearing that you have a "bona fide intent to use" the mark at some time in the future. Or, if you prefer, you can wait until you have actually used the mark on the product in commerce and then apply based on "actual use." In an "intent to use" case, the date of first use relates to the date of filing, so that even if someone actually uses the mark in commerce before you but you file first, you win! At some point you will use the mark and submit a "statement of use" with a specimen of the mark as used in commerce—a label on the clothes or an ad for the dry cleaning services, for example. Once approved, the mark will be registered! The process usually takes about a year, but since your rights attach from first use or filing, it really doesn't matter how long they take at the Trademark Office. I will say this: The trademark examining attorneys at the U.S. Patent and Trademark Office are some of the most professional, efficient, and pleasant federal bureaucrats I have ever worked with!

Once the Mark Is Registered, What Happens?

Federal registrations last for 10 years and are renewable forever as long as you continue using the mark. However, during the first 10-year period you must submit an affidavit of continued use between the fifth and sixth years or the mark will be abandoned. This seems like an annoying necessity so soon after getting a registration. Still, the truth is that many new businesses don't make it to the 5-year point, and if the mark becomes abandoned it will be available to others who might wish to register it.

Six months before the end of the first 10-year period you have to tell the Trademark Office that you are still using your mark and show them how (i.e., provide them with a specimen of the mark as used); they will then renew it for another 10 years and so on, forever!

The registration and the subsequent maintenance of marks do not require that you hire a lawyer. Nonetheless, because your brand is so valuable, a prudent plan includes a lawyer review and oversight even if you do not pay a lawyer to handle the overall registration process.

Keeping Your Advertising Ideas (After All, You Paid for Them!)

Advertising is ubiquitous in business. Businesses create new ads for old stuff, for new stuff, and for not-yet-developed stuff. My MBA education taught me that good advertising can make even a dead dog hunt! Businesses create lots of things that are protectable by copyright and that aren't advertising, as we will discuss more fully hereafter; but advertising is a target-rich environment with which to begin the discussion of how to keep this type of intellectual property as your own.

A "Career Case" Example of Copyright Law at Work

"This is it!" I thought. "A career case for sure!" (For all you non-lawyers, a "career case" is a case that makes, and hopefully ends, your legal career by allowing you to retire to the lap of luxury in the Colorado Rockies!) Angel, the young widow who sat in my office, actually cried as she explained that the only legacy her late husband had left her and their children were the rights to some software that he had created for MOBIL Oil Company. The case, just like Mary Poppins, was practically perfect in every way! The client (the "Widow Angel" no less) was sympathetic and presentable, the defendant had lots and lots of money, and the facts and the law were on my side! The "Widow Angel" case, as it is still referred to in my home, turned out to be a career case lesson in humility. We got poured out (more lawyer vernacular, meaning "we lost") at the trial court level, never even making it to a jury, and the appeal went no better. So much for the perfect case. As I am now fond of saying, there is a reason David and Goliath is such a good story. The reason is that nine times out of 10, Goliath pounds the stew out of David!

What does this have to do with advertising, you might be asking yourself. Well, the "Widow Angel" case and the rights to your advertising both hinge on a nuance of the copyright law that you need to know about. Here's how it works: You hire a person to create an ad for your company. This person has her own advertising business. You pay her for the ad she creates. You own the copyright to the ad, correct? *Wrong.* "The Law" is not always logical. In fact, it is often illogical. That's why there are law schools! In this case, the law says that when you hire an "independent contractor," meaning a person who has his or her own business, this person is considered the "author" of the ad and the owner of the copyright to it! Even though you paid for it! Huh? Yep. In the "Widow Angel" case, I was not able to prove that the software Mobil Oil was using was software that the "Widow Angel's" husband had written as an independent contractor while he had his own business, so I lost the case.

You will lose too if you try to use the ad you paid for beyond the terms agreed to with the ad company. That is, even though you paid for the ad, the ad company owns the copyright to it, and you can use the ad only for the time and purpose stipulated by the parties—your fall advertising campaign, for example. Then, if the ad goes great and you want to use it again, guess what. You have to get permission from the ad company to do so! They may cut you a deal, but because they own the copyright, they have the right to prevent you from using "your ad" without their permission. Ouch! In order for you to own the copyright to an ad you pay someone to create, you need to add this highly technical intellectual property verbiage to the contract for services: "And, furthermore, wherein the party of the first part, known to me as a party person of the very highest order…" Nah, I'm just kidding. Here is all you need to add to ensure that you own what you are paying someone else to create: "[*The Ad Company*] hereby transfers the copyrights in the ad to [*You*]." That's all that is required, a simple transfer of ownership in writing.

Often, when a company is asked to transfer the ownership in writing, the representative will say, "OK, but that will cost more!" And this is when you say, "Good-bye. There are thousands of ad companies in this town!" And the ad company rep will say, "OK, wait. For you we will do a special deal." Whatever the representative says, the point is not to pay the company if you don't get the copyright ownership in writing first!

And here is another thing you should get in writing from the independent contractors you hire: a guarantee that the work they create for you and for which you are paying them is *original*. Copyrights attach for "original" works of art and authorship only. When the ad company copies something off the Internet (and you would be surprised at the number of people who think it is OK to copy something just because it is easy to copy!) and you have run the ad for a day and then get a nasty letter from Chicago saying, "Stop! That is our ad!" you can work the problem out with the people in Chicago and then turn around and "work it out" with your former ad company.

In summary, when you hire a person with his or her own business to create any ad for you, you want two things: a written transfer of the copyrights and a guarantee that whatever the person sells you is original work.

What Is a "Work For Hire" and Why Should You Care?

Asked why he felt that his client was free to copy the movie, the defendant's lawyer said, "Well, because, Judge, that movie got no FBI warning on it!" (This is a true story, I swear, from a real case I observed—not mine—in Austin, Texas, in the mid-1980s.) In this case, the old saying "Ignorance of the law is no excuse" played out to a predictable, sad (rhymes with "bad") conclusion. You also need to know what the law says a "work for hire" is, because, in fact, ignorance is no excuse!

You might think that when you hire someone to do some work for you, that that is a "work for hire." That would seem logical, but it is *wrong*. As we discussed above, the law is often not logical, and if the person you hire owns the business, it is not a "work for hire" under the copyright laws. Instead, that person with his or her own business is termed an "independent contractor" and owns the copyrights to the original work you paid the business to create.

If, on the other hand, the person you hire to do work is an *employee* of yours when they create any original work of art or authorship for you, you own the copyright because the copyright law says that this is a "work for hire."

So the way this plays out is, you hire creative folks and put together your own ad department for your company. Then you say, "Create some ads." Now, because this constitutes a "work for hire" situation, the company owns the copyrights, period. No additional transfer in writing is required.

You should want to know this information because it will make your life easier when it comes time to fight the bad guys who stole your great idea for an ad. What kind of nasty letter from Chicago will you be able to write if you don't have a clue who created what ad for you when? The point of knowing the rules is knowing what kind of leverage you have when confronted by evildoers! So how do you protect these original works of art and authorship that you now know how to own?

Free Steps to Protect Your Ads

It can be safely said that creative, artsy-craftsy people and lawyers go together about as well as oil and water. Creative people need lawyers from time to time, but the two groups just don't seem to hang out in the same joints! Anyway, it used to be the law that if an artist painted a picture or an author wrote a top ten hit and did not put a copyright notice on it, they lost the copyright! As you can imagine, a lot of early, creative work got lost to the public because of ignorance of this law, and it made creative people mad. Luckily, that is no longer the law! The good news is that now, once you reduce an ad to a tangible form (i.e., save it to your hard drive, print it out, etc.), it is protected *for free* under the copyright law without you having to do anything else! That is correct: All you have to do is create an original ad and print it out, and it is protected under the copyright laws. And if you can prove you own it, you can stop other people from copying it! No filing fees, no lawyer fees, nothing!

Here is a better business practice tip: It is true what I just said; you do not have to put the copyright notice (i.e., the word "copyright" or the symbol ©, the year of first publication, and the owner's name) on your original ad. My tip is, put it on anyway! It will be a whole lot easier to prove it is yours if it has your name on it, don't you think?

Anyway, that is all you have to do to protect your original works of art and/or authorship, and it costs nothing! Here is the downside to free, however: It leaves you with less leverage and harder options. By that I mean that in order to enforce this copyright, you must be able to prove you own it and you must be able to prove you were damaged by the copying of your ad by the bad guy. Proving copyright damages is a very difficult thing to do in most cases. On the one hand, if the ad is working, you are making more money than ever. On the other hand, if it is not working, the defendant says, "Judge, that was the worst ad I ever copied. I mean, I lost money running that ad. He should pay me for copying his stupid ad!" Wouldn't it be nice if you could show the judge a document instantly creating the presumption that you owned the ad and that meant you could assert a claim for damages even though you couldn't prove you were damaged at all? Sounds good to me, little grasshopper! Let's find out how to get such a document.

Maximum Protection for Your Ads: Time and Cost

When it comes time to count the cost-benefit advantage of a certificate of copyright registration, I believe that it is, pound for pound (or in the United States, penny for penny), the best investment you can make if you want to maximize your protection under the copyright laws. A copyright registration lasts for your lifetime plus 70 years or, as a corporate asset, 95 years from creation or 125 years from publication, whichever is less. That is a good long time in the general scheme of things. Also, once issued, it is accepted by the courts as rebuttable evidence of ownership, and best of all, it lets you have the following discussion with the judge: "Judge, we don't have a clue how much this guy has damaged us by copying our ad, but we do know that we registered it and the only difference is that he whited out our copyright notice. We ask for maximum statutory damages in the amount of $150,000 per infringement plus our court costs and Shaffer's million dollars in attorney's fees. Thank you very much."

"Well, that sounds pretty good," you say, "but what's the cost to get one of these copyright registrations? I mean, free is good." OK, I hear that, so how does $30 grab you? That is the total fee for filing a copyright application for your original ad. The process usually takes about six months or so to complete. So the analysis you must do is, how does $30 stack up against the cost of the ad? Since no self-respecting ad company is going to begin work on your ad campaign for less than $60,000, $30 sounds like a good investment to me! You might skip the expense for a one-page flyer you put out for a one-day show. But if the ad costs more than $30 to create, then I would seriously consider spending $30 to maximize protection of your great idea under copyright law. You might even spring for an hour or two of a lawyer's time to have it done for you! (See Chapter 4 and Appendix C for more information about copyrights.)

What Are Trade Secrets and Do You Have Any?

About every six months or so a client will ask me about patenting a recipe for chili or gumbo or gumbo chili, and I will say, "Not unless it cures cancer." Otherwise, the only protection for cooking recipes is to keep them secret. Think about the formula for COCA-COLA or KENTUCKY FRIED CHICKEN, for example. These two recipes are the extraordinarily valuable and jealously guarded foundations of two big-time players in the business world. PEPSI and CHURCH'S would dearly love to know exactly what goes into that other soda and chicken to make them taste like they do. Why? Because they taste good! They are selling a lot of soda and chicken, and it sure wouldn't hurt to know how they do it. The point is that the secret recipes of COKE and KFC give them a competitive advantage. And that is just what your trade secrets do for you! Now I can hear you saying that you are just a little company and that you don't have any valuable trade secrets. Wrong! Do you have a sourcing plan, a pricing strategy, or a customer list you keep internally and don't share with the public? If so, you have "trade secrets." In short, a trade secret is anything of competitive value that you know, and your competitors would like to know, that makes you money or saves you money. How you are making money when they are not? With your "tricks of the trade." You have them; every business does. Keeping your secrets yours is the trick. But first, here is an example of what *not* to do.

Protecting Your Competitive Edge

"The Japanese are coming! The Japanese are coming!" This was the frightened refrain that ran through corporate America in the early 1980s. It seemed then that the mighty Japanese electronic juggernaut was about to reduce America's competitive edge to zip. America's response to this perceived threat was remarkable. Twenty of America's high-tech electronics companies agreed to band together as one to try to salvage the day. Even more remarkably, they agreed that the members of this group would share whatever technology they jointly developed. Thus, MCC, the Microelectronics and Computer Technology Consortium, was born, and it picked a sleepy little college town in the middle of Texas as its home. That was, some say, the start of the rise of Austin, Texas, as "Silicon Hills," and those were exciting and happy times. Not too much later, the Japanese tiger was found to be made of paper and the threat evaporated. Perhaps that is why MCC hired a person who had signed a trade secret agreement with StakTek Corporation. MCC knew of the contract the person had signed limiting what he could work on, and they hired him and had him work on it anyway! Some time after a multimillion-dollar judgment against them, MCC members decided they had had enough fun and disbanded! Unless you have lots of extra millions lying around, you definitely do not want to do what they did!

Free Steps to Protect Your Trade Secrets

"First, get yourself a Lone Star!" (That was my favorite ad when we lived in Texas. It was the punchline to the beer ad that said stuff like "How to make great Bar-B-Q!" Whenever I get a home repair project sprung on me, it is still my favorite starting gambit!) With regard to trade secrets, first figure out what they are! Make a list. Start a file. Keep it secret. Limit what other people know about them on a "need to know" basis. Do they really need to know this secret to do their jobs? If not, don't tell them! When I first started my own law firm in 1984, I believed that every new employee would be with me until I passed away writing patent applications. In a very short time, I realized no one stays that long. Some only stay a day! You who have your own businesses also know this is true. So don't tell your employees your secrets unless they need to know them to do their jobs.

Make a List and Keep It Secret

Next, actually make a list of the things that are your trade secrets. This does not need to include the entire trade secret but merely an identifying description. This is an edifying and rewarding thing to do. You will be surprised how long your list is when you take the time to compile the competitive advantages you've learned over the years. The actual trade secrets the list identifies may be maintained in your office in a lock box or some other convenient and safe location, such as an off-site computer.

Educate Your Employees

Next, educate your employees about trade secrets and impress upon them the vital value of these great ideas to your business ("Loose lips sink ships" and so forth). While you are doing this, have them agree that they will not disclose these secrets to anyone outside the company.

I am now going to teach you two sayings that will make people think you are a lawyer. First, whenever you are asked a question that you do not know the answer to, pause, look up at the ceiling and then back at the person asking the question, and say, "It depends." Second, whenever someone says, "How about coming over for dinner?" you say, "Put it in writing!"

The point is, while these free steps to protect your trade secrets we have just discussed are important and should be taken if you want to have any chance of protecting your trade secrets, the better policy is to "get it in writing." Why?

Because people forget, people change their minds, people lose their minds, but paper never changes. What kind of paper do you need? Read on!

Maximum Protection for Your Trade Secrets: Time and Cost

All of the various forms of intellectual property are designed to protect your great idea legally from your competitors. With regard to trade secrets, the competitor you are protecting yourself against tomorrow is your most valuable employee today! Maximum protection will require a lawyer to draft or approve a written employment agreement. There is a lot of confusion as to what should be in a good employment agreement when it comes to control over an ex-employee!

Non-Compete Agreement = Starvation

The most common form of protection I see used by employers is the so called non-compete agreement. "You'll never work in this business again anywhere in the world for the rest of your life": This is the kind of non-compete agreement most employers feel is appropriate. The problem is that while employers can fire employees, courts generally frown on giving an employer the unlimited right to stop an ex-employee from doing what he or she is trained to do. As a result, even if an employee signed an employment contract with a non-compete agreement as broad as the one above, a court would "reform" the language to be "reasonable" in "scope" and "duration." If an employer sued to enforce such an agreement, the court could say that "anywhere in the world" means "this county" and "for the rest of your life" means "for another 30 minutes." You see, non-compete agreements are about *starvation*. No judge is going to allow an employer to fire a former employee and then starve him or her to death. So while I don't tell employers to take the non-compete agreement out of their employment contracts, I do tell them not to expect that they will be enforced as written. I also tell them to add a trade secret agreement to the contract if they really want some teeth in it. Why?

Trade Secret Agreements = Stealing

This is how it works. For employees you are thinking of hiring, you tell them that you will teach them all the tricks of the trade you know. You tell them that these tricks are your trade secrets and nobody outside of your business knows them. Then you tell them that they will have to agree in writing to one of two options when hired. Option A: We get to give you a lobotomy when you decide to leave. Sign here. Option B: You agree not to take the trade secrets with you when you leave and use them against the company. Sign here. Pretty much all your employees will take option B. Then, when they leave in the dead of night (because they always leave in the dead of night) and open a competing Web site and send a "10 percent off" e-mail to all your clients, you can sue them to enforce your trade secret agreement. And a breach of a trade secret agreement is about *stealing*! I am telling you as a lawyer, every court in America, even in California, still agrees that stealing is bad behavior. It's that simple! (In fact, a good company motto would be "The simpler the better when we go to court.") So right away the judge is on your side. You say, "Judge, yesterday I was in here about starvation, but today I am here about stealing! That person stole from me." And the judge says, "That's bad" and you say, "Yes it is, and what is worse, he signed this agreement right here that says he wouldn't do what he just did, and that is his signature!" And the judge says, "Guilty. Pay a lot of money. Next case." It's over, you won, and you could probably win it without even having to pay your lawyer to get off the golf course and help. You should pay your lawyer to prepare a proper trade secret addendum for your employment agreement, but that is about it. A minimal cost and time investment, for sure, to protect your great trade secret ideas.

This is an example of the powerful leverage you get by using intellectual property law to protect your great idea—leverage, as I have said, that will enable you to end those inevitable conflicts that arise with every successful business quickly, inexpensively, and in your favor!

Pre- and Post-Employment Interviews

Now for a few closing thoughts for businesses. As part of the prospective employee interview process, always ask for copies of the applicant's previous employment contracts. This way you will find out what type of trade secret agreements they have already signed, since you sure don't want to be the next MCC. Likewise, assuming you get notice when employees are leaving, always conduct an exit interview where you reiterate the trade secret agreement they have signed, maybe even having them sign an agreement that they re-read it and that they understand that they are not to use your trade secrets in the new job!

3

Free Protection for Your Great Invention

From the magnificent, heavier-than-air flying machine to the mundane paper clip, life in the United States is about innovation! This chapter will guide the inventor in you through the twisted paths from conception to commercialization of a great idea and explain how to keep total control over it all the while!

First Things First: Great Ideas Are Hard to Appreciate

What would you say the chances are that the son of an itinerant barber would hit it big in the business world? Even in the United States (the only country in the world, by the way, where the overlaid first two letters of its name is the symbol for its currency!) I would have to say the chances would be slim. Nonetheless, just such a person, Chester Carlson, put together a prototype of a business machine in his wife's kitchen. (Don't you know she was happy about that!) Once the prototype proved itself, Chester got not one but several patents for the new device. Then he took them to business companies all over the country and showed them what it could do, seeking to sell it to them. What was their response? Nothing. Not even as smart a company as International Business Machines could see much use for it. So Chester hit the venture capital market, and they took a flyer on it and formed a start-up company. They called it XEROX Corporation. What a country! The point here is that even revolutionary, "pioneering" ideas are hard for people to appreciate. The future, even when it is right in front of you, under your nose and in your office, is very hard to see. Those of you reading this who have a great idea that may be patentable are a worried group. What do you have to do to secure the rights to your great idea, and how many millions will it cost? Those are your nervous questions, but here are the happy answers.

The First, Free Steps to Protect Your Great Idea for an Invention

I don't think Americans are the most inventive group of people the world has ever seen because we are smarter than everybody else. I believe we are so inventive because our laws favor inventors, both the big guys and the little guys, more than those of other countries. The truth is that the big guys, the Hewlett-Packards and IBMs of the world, don't care what the laws are. What I mean is, they have all the intellectual property attorneys they will ever need, and they can handle whatever obstacles to protecting their ideas may come their way. For the little guy, though, the rules matter a lot. It amuses me that every time the political season heats up you hear "The independent inventor is the backbone of American industry!" That is true, I believe, but once the election is over, the politicians seem to forget this and start "harmonizing" our laws to conform with the rest of the world. It seems to me that when you hear the word "harmonize," it usually means that some good deal for the little guy in America just got taken away. Here is how to use the rules to your advantage and protect your great idea for free!

First to Invent: One Very Good Rule

What is one rule that favors the inventor in the United States that hasn't yet been harmonized away? One very good one is this: When two inventors come up with the same idea in the United States, unlike the rest of the world, it is not a race to the Patent Office that determines who wins. In the United States we have a rule that favors the little guy: The person who invented first wins! How cool is that! If you live in Canada and come up with a great idea you want to patent, you have to rush out and spend your retirement or college savings on a patent application today, because if someone invents the same thing tomorrow and files before you, you lose! Ouch! Good law for patent attorneys, bad law for inventors.

Now, the "first to invent" rule does have its issues. You will have to be able to prove you had your great idea first. Well, how do you prove that? How do you prove anything? Typically, the person with the best "tangible" evidence wins. If the best the other guy has got is his mom on the stand saying, "Billy invented this five years ago" and you have a signed, witnessed, dated document disclosing your great idea for an invention in confidence, who is the judge or jury going to believe? No offense to Billy's mom.

The answer, then, to what you have to do to protect your great idea for an invention, is to be the first to make a written record of it and get it witnessed, and that costs nothing! No lawyer required! First to invent rules, first to file drools, baby!

A Simple Written Disclosure Is the Key

You might be asking, what is it that gets witnessed? It is what I call a "Confidential Proprietary Invention Disclosure Document" (see Appendix B for a copy of the one I give my clients), probably because that title includes about every relevant intellectual property law word possible. It really can be called anything you like, and it will serve the purpose of creating evidence of the date of your invention. No matter what you call it, the form should answer at least the following three questions: What is the problem? What have other people done to solve the problem up to now so far as you know? What have you done that is so neat? You should attach sketches if you have them. That's it. The form I use includes other questions that provide me with information that may be useful, such as the inventor's name, address, date of conception of the idea, etc. The most important part of the form, however, is the part for the two witnesses to sign and date. It says, "Witnesses: After *first* agreeing to keep this information confidential, I have read and understand the above disclosure."

It is probably best not to have your mom or wife or five-year-old sign it, since that doesn't look too strong. Any friend or other person who can actually understand the invention and who *first* agrees to keep your great idea confidential will do.

Keep Your Great Idea Confidential

That agreement to keep your great idea confidential is a very big deal and points up another reason the United States is such fertile ground for innovation. Everywhere else on the planet, the little guy must base his decision to invest in a patent application on his mom's evaluation of the market. Well, I don't know about you, but my mom (God rest her beautiful soul) loved every goofy idea I ever had. "Nevie, look at those mud pies! You're a genius!" Again, the big guys don't care what the rules are because they have all the money, so they don't have to rely on their mom so much. But here's the rule: In every other country in the world, if an inventor offers the product for sale to see if there really is a market like Mom says, and the inventor didn't first spend the money to file a patent application, the product's not patentable! It's not "new" under their cheesy systems, and if it's not new, it's not patentable. In the United States, however, you can actually put your product on the market and see how it does before deciding to spend the money on a patent application. In the United States, it is still considered "new" and you have one year from the date you offer to sell your invention in which to determine whether or not to file a patent application.

So if you don't care about foreign patents (more about the siren song of foreign patents later), you have a year in the United States after you make a non-confidential disclosure of your idea within which to start the patent process. But a year is only a year, and you do not want to start the clock any sooner than you have to. So the second basic thing you need to do with your great idea, after getting a written witnessed disclosure, is *keep it confidential* as long as possible.

My First Inventor

I usually don't have to encourage a client's paranoia, but it is safe to say that it sure helps your chances of making something from your great idea if you don't go blabbing it all over the place. Which reminds me of the very first inventor who came to my office. He looked like a cartoon caricature of an inventor. He had a trench coat on, wore big, dark-rimmed glasses, and carried a brown, rumpled paper bag tightly in both hands. (All he was lacking was a beanie cap with a propeller blade!) He sat down and looked at me and I looked at him across my brand new patent attorney desk. (We weren't calling ourselves intellectual property lawyers yet.) I said something snappy like "So, you've invented something?" And he said, "Yes. It is something that will put the oil companies out of business." And I said, "Wow! Tell me about it!" And he said, "Oh, I can't tell you about it because if I tell you what it is, the oil companies will kill you." And I said, "I really do appreciate your concern for my health, but if you can't tell me what it is you invented, I can't help you!" And he walked out, and the oil companies are still in business, and I don't know what that means.

So, again, making a written record of your idea and getting it witnessed is step 1. Step 2 is keeping your great idea confidential as long as possible. Ah, but this is a "catch-22" of sorts, is it not? Inventors really need to tell some people about their great idea—prototype manufacturers, investors, and such. But now you know you can't because it will start the one-year clock ticking. But you really want to tell this particular person. What do you do?

Non-disclosure/Confidentiality Agreement: "Critical Tool"

The way out of this dilemma is a written agreement called a "Non-disclosure Agreement" or a "Non-disclosure Confidentiality Agreement." I like the second description better because it says what the person who signs will and won't do. They *will not* disclose the information you provide to them, and they *will* keep the information you impart to them confidential. There are as many forms of NDAs (cool lawyer slang for what we are discussing right now) as there are whitewater rapids in Idaho. The basic elements are simple, however: Part 1: I, the person with the Great Idea, agree to disclose my Great Idea concerning an anti-gravity device to you, Big Company. Part 2: Big Company agrees to review my anti-gravity device for the purpose of making a prototype, manufacturing and marketing it, or buying it outright. Part 3: Big Company agrees not to disclose my Great Idea and to keep my Great Idea confidential for ten thousand years.

I should tell you that the number one request I get when it comes to drafting any contract whatsoever is "Keep it simple; one page will do." This can be done with NDAs but know this: The big company's 37-page, small-print, front-and-back NDA is *not* simple because every paragraph in it represents some horrible thing that happened to them and that, "by gosh and golly," will not happen again. So NDAs don't have to be long and complicated, but be sure to get your intellectual property lawyer to look over the one you download off the Internet or be ready to add a paragraph or two to it when you get the next Great Idea. (See Appendix B for a sample NDA.)

What Are NDAs Really?

NDAs are a simple, usually very inexpensive way for you to show your great idea to people without losing any legal rights to your idea and without giving the people who sign the NDA any legal rights to the idea. What they are not is a gun. After somebody, person or company, signs an NDA and you show them your anti-gravity device, can they steal it? Why, yes they can! It's stealing. Someone who steals, by definition, has no respect for legal contracts! So I suggest the military strategy of "need to know." Even if people sign the NDA, disclose to them only what they need to know. Keep something in reserve. Because, you know, there are some bad people in the world who will sign legal documents and then take your great idea anyway! Again, the NDA is just a piece of paper, not a gun. Still, if a company does sign a proper NDA and then steals your idea, you can sue them for breach of contract and maybe get more money than they were ever willing to pay you legally for the idea. (I am trying to be optimistic here!)

Who Will Sign an NDA?

The short answer is anybody you pay will sign an NDA. The people you are likely to pay are usually prototype manufacturers or specialists you hire to help work out the details of your great idea for an invention. They are in business to help people with great ideas, and because you are going to pay them they will sign the NDA. They will often have their own NDA because all patent attorneys have instructed their inventors to tell people about their idea only after they sign an NDA. Bottom line: They want your money, not your great idea.

Beware of the Invention Development Company on TV

A subgroup of people who will sign an NDA are the folks who run so-called invention development companies. *Be very careful about using these companies.* They usually run ads on TV late at night that say stuff like "Wake up! Surely even a slug like you has had a great idea at some time. Call now and we'll make you rich!" The truth is, these companies are in the business of making someone rich, but it is not you. They are *not* in the "make you rich" business. They are in the flattery business, and while they are patting you on the back for your great idea ("Pink paper clips! What a great idea! Do you know how many paper clips were sold last year? Why, if you only got 10 percent of the market, you could retire to the lap of luxury in Redmond, Washington, and have famous neighbors!") they are digging around in your back pocket for your wallet. They promise to get your great idea in front of their "business contacts" and to help you with a "marketing plan." This typically translates to sending a canned pitch to a bunch of companies that wish they could sign up on a "No Spam" list to prevent such incoming trash. Some do more than others, and the odds are that there is probably at least one honest invention development company out there. But think about it a moment. How likely is it that a single company can take every person's idea that comes to them and make each of those people rich? It is hard enough for companies that actually have a successful product to stay focused and profitable. "NEW COKE" comes to mind. I mean, what were they thinking? They had a great product; it was selling like gangbusters, so the obvious thing to do is change it! Oh well.

I have had quite a few clients who just weren't comfortable with the invention development company pitch. My advice to them, and to you if you are thinking of working with one and want to know if it is legitimate, is to ask them this question: Would you please send me a list of the top 100 folks you have made rich? I predict that the company will say that such information is confidential. So you tell them that you do not want current clients—certainly, that information is confidential—but just folks who have retired filthy rich; let's say just the top ten. How about just one? When they refuse to give you even one name, you'll know what business they are really in. But, they will sign an NDA! Why? Because they do not care about your great idea! They are not going to steal your great idea for pink paper clips. They just want your money! (Despite all my years as a patent attorney, I cannot name a single reputable invention development company to which to refer my clients. That should tell you a lot!)

Who Won't Sign an NDA?

So who won't sign an NDA? Just about every other company or person you might want to talk to. These companies are the ones you hope will buy your great idea. The problem is, they are busy trying to make a living, and your letter or e-mail is just a nuisance to them. Usually, all you will get back, if you get back anything at all, is a polite letter saying that it is their company policy not to take ideas from outside. They may also send you a "Non-confidentiality Disclosure Document" for you to sign if you persist in trying to talk to them about your great idea. Stop and re-read that last sentence. I actually had a client ask me, "What do you think it means?" I think it means what it says. Anything you tell them under that agreement is *not* confidential. Oops! (Here is another lawyer tip: When it comes to contracts or life in general, if you do not understand it, do not sign it! Make your lawyer explain it and keep explaining it until you understand it, or forget it! The invasion of Normandy was a pretty complicated deal, but it can be explained pretty simply. The same is true for every legal document you ever need to sign!)

Now, some companies may sign a proper NDA, but you should not count on it. Still, it is a good place to start the dialogue, and it does not put your idea in jeopardy because you haven't told them any details of your great idea! So it doesn't hurt to ask!

As a last point, your lawyer is the one person on the planet you do not need to have sign an NDA. The law imposes a duty on all lawyers to keep whatever you tell them confidential even without an NDA. Think "attorney-client privilege." My advice, however, is to treat your lawyer just like everyone else: Don't tell your lawyer anything until you need to! You can have a very satisfying conversation with your lawyer about your great idea for an invention without spilling your guts. Your lawyer will tell you when he or she needs more information in order to help you!

What Do You Do If They Won't Sign an NDA?

One of my favorite movies is *Cannery Row,* with Nick Nolte and Debra Winger. There is a scene in the movie when Nolte is puzzling over how to light up his fish tank with some octopi he caught so he can watch what they do and write a paper on it. The head of the local layabouts comes in and asks Nolte what he is doing, and Nolte tells him. Well, the bum spends two or three seconds max looking in the tank and then utters these words of wisdom: "Why don't you just give up?"

People with great ideas should remember these words because sometimes they represent the best course of action! If companies won't sign an NDA, one option is to give up—not on your great idea, but on the idea that someone else is going to make you rich. We will discuss other options and avenues for making money on your great idea later on, but for now all you need to know is to make a written record of your great idea and keep it confidential. Neither step costs a dime, and you will have done all you need to do to protect the idea as your own, at least to a minimum degree, while you decide what to do next. So what do you do next? My advice is to use the greatest economic opportunity equalizer the world has ever seen. Get thee to the Internet!

Research the Commercial Viability of Your Great Idea

It used to be that if you weren't John D. Rockefeller and you didn't already have all the money, buildings, and lawyers in the world, there was no way you were ever going to compete with an established business. Now, however, you have the Internet. I believe that we are just beginning to grasp what the Internet is going to do to revolutionize our lives. I can practice law in the most beautiful city in the world, next to the prettiest beach in the world and stay in contact with clients in all 50 states and all over the world. What a world! And you with the great idea can research the market for your idea from the comfort and privacy of your own home! It is pretty obvious that the more information you have about the market in which your great idea is going to operate, the better able you will be to decide whether or not to spend any money on the idea.

While I was living in Texas, I would ask my clients if they had done any research on the market for their idea. They would say, "Yep. The market is big." And I would say, "Great. So you have researched the market. How big is it?" And they would say, "Dang Big!" You know, I love Texans, my two children are Texans, but sometimes…Anyway, my point is, you need to know as much *specific* information about the market as you can possibly know, and GOOGLE is your very best friend. You can start a research file for your great idea that includes the top 100 companies in the field, what their revenues were for the last ten years, what their current best seller is, and so forth. You want to know more than their own salespeople do about the market. Why? Because, knowledge is indeed power. If the total market for your great idea is $50, forget about spending any money on trying to protect it!

By spending time researching the market, you will also discover where in the world Carmen San Diego is. (Just kidding.) You will learn where your market is, and that is a very important thing to know. Where your market is tells you where you need to protect your great idea and where you should get a patent, if that is your decision. And here is *a great big tip: Forget about patents in countries run by dictators!* By definition, dictators do not care what the law is and give no credence to legal documents, such as patents, unless their brother owns them. A common mistake inventors make is to assume they need protection in the places where the product will be manufactured and/or knocked off. This is *wrong*! You need to protect the product only in the country or countries where it will be sold. And here is the good news: The United States is the best market in the world for everything! That's what we do. What did the president say after the tragedy of 9/11? "Go shopping!" (That still echoes in my mind. But Americans work long and hard, and I guess if the reason we do that is so we can spend our hard-earned dollars on "stuff," so be it!) The point is, if all you ever wanted for your great idea is the best market in the world, you are living in the right place if you are living in the United States!

Three Free Folders

So now you have three folders for each great idea. Folder one has your signed, witnessed Invention Disclosure document; folder two has all the signed Non-disclosure Agreements you have entered into; and folder three has your market research. Best of all, there is no rush, no fuss, and no fees!

What Does a Big Company Really Mean When They Say, "Come Back When You Have a Patent?"

It is not infrequently that clients rush to my office excited by a conversation they have had with a company that they think would be a good match for their great idea. They are very anxious to hire me to file a patent application right away for them. When I ask them what the hurry is, they say, "The company says to come back and talk to them when I have a patent!" Well, my law license says "Attorney and Counselor at Law," and with my counselor hat on I say, "Do you want to know what they mean by that before you spend a lot of money on a patent application that may never turn into a patent?" And before they can say no, I tell them that what the company is really saying is "Go away and never come back!" You see, a patent is a public document that you and they and anyone else can pull up at the Patent Office Web site (www.uspto.gov) any time they want. If you ever get a patent, they will see it, and if they want to see you, they will call you! Otherwise, they never want to see you again. Why, you may ask, is this so? Well, I think it is because it is difficult to make a living, and the company you talked to has figured out a way to make some money and has invested heavily in that way, and they do not care to hear about your great new idea. Further, they already have plenty of folks working on their current stuff, and they are not going to stop and listen to you! They are, in fact, invested in yesterday! This is more true the bigger the company is. Who are you to tell *them* that *their* product is out of date? The last buggy whip manufacturer was saying this at the exact moment a horseless carriage ran over him and put him out of business. Sad, isn't it? But, you might say, isn't it true what the politicians say when they are running for office, that it is the little guy who is the backbone of innovation in this country? Yes, I believe it is true; it's just that the little guy should not expect to get any help whatsoever from the big guy. The big guys are trying hard to make themselves rich, and they really have no time to spend or interest in making you rich. No offense!

Do You Have to Do a Patent Search?

One of the other things you can do while you are waiting for someone to sign an NDA is more research! I am often asked what a patent search costs and, like a good lawyer, I reply, "It depends." First I tell my clients that there is no law that requires you to do a patent search. So you can skip the search altogether and spend nothing at all. Or you can spend the gross domestic product of the United States on a patent search, and even if you spent every dime on the planet you would still not know "for sure" if your great idea is patentable. Any patent search is, at best, no more than a "go/no-go" decision-making tool. The reason for this is that a large number of patent applications that are pending at the U.S. Patent Office are confidential and may never be searched. So the fact is, even if you spent every dime on the planet on a search, some other guy in North Carolina may have had the same idea and filed before you. The only way you would ever know this is if you filed a patent application yourself. Then the patent examiner would say, "Hey, we have two applications for the same anti-gravity device." Now, remember, in every other country in the world, you would be dead. The first to file wins everywhere in the world, except in the United States. In the United States the issue is, who invented it first? Here the patent examiner will declare an "Interference," and the person who has the best evidence that they invented the great idea first wins! (This, in my personal experience, does not happen very often. In all my years of practice I have never been involved in an Interference proceeding. Just thought you'd like to know!) If you already have the written, witnessed invention disclosure discussed above, you have a big leg up on any competition lacking that tangible evidence!

Can You Do a Patent Search Yourself?

I do fewer "formal" searches for my clients these days because they do their own! Thanks to the Internet, inventors can go online and search the very large number of U.S. patent records available there for free! Pardon me while I say this again: What a country! (See Appendix B, where I walk you through a patent search.) The problem is that, even though it's free, patent searching is more of an art than a science. Don't believe me? Go there and type in "Dog" and "Bowl," and you will see what I am talking about. Now, even though it is true that the U.S. Patent and Trademark Office (USPTO) search is a powerful, free tool and you can do a patent search yourself, it is also true that if you have never done one, you won't know if the search was good or bad. And if you have never read a patent before, how likely is it that you will be able to accurately say what a patent covers? Certainly, the U.S. patents are written in English and they usually have pictures that help show what great idea the inventor tried to protect. But if you do not know what the "claims" of a patent are, you will not be able to understand the limits of the patent. I will explain the "claims" in a little bit, but my advice if you do your own search is to take the results to your patent attorney and let him or her tell you what it means. Just pick out the patents that look closest to your great idea and then find out if they really are by letting your patent attorney tell you!

As to the difficulty of finding patents that are even close to your invention, the good news is that there are people who actually make a living doing professional searches. They are sort of like those Internet gurus who know the magic tricks to getting your Web site high on the search engine lists. Professional search firms know how to do a search that is meaningful but not exorbitant. Whenever a client asks me to conduct a formal search, I use a "search firm" from which I have a signed NDA. I send them an outline of the great idea. They then do a human- and computer-aided search of actual U.S. patent records and send me a stack of a dozen or so patents along with an invoice for about $500. I then spend my time reviewing the patents and comparing them against my understanding of your great idea. Then I prepare a legal opinion letter telling my client what I think the search means, if it looks good or bad, and why. And I send my client the results of the search so that my client can review them too, and then we can talk. The total cost for a simple search these days is usually around $1,500.

What If Your Exact Idea Shows Up in the Patent Search?

Usually, the search leaves some of your great idea available for protection and some of it exposed as old stuff. Sometimes the exact same great idea shows up in another guy's patent. That is bad news as far as you getting a patent. After something has been patented once, it can never be patented again. That idea is officially old, not new, and it is never patentable again. This is true even if it never made it to the marketplace and no one outside the Patent Office ever knew of it. The good news is that at least you didn't spend any money on a patent application. And another positive thing is that the patent might have expired. Patents only last something less than 20 years, and once they expire, anyone can make, use, or sell the previously patented thing. So you might find out you can't get a patent, but your research shows that your great idea still has commercial legs. Now you're in the hamburger business! By that I mean that there's no patent on a hamburger, but McDONALD'S couldn't care less, and they are still selling billions of burgers. See Chapter 2 and Chapter 4 for what to do to protect your idea without a patent.

Summary of Free Steps

OK, now you know how to protect your great anti-gravity invention idea for free. Make a written record and get it witnessed; keep your great idea confidential as long as possible, and tell people about it only after they have signed a proper Non-disclosure/Confidentiality Agreement; and research the commercial viability of the idea on the Internet, including possible patent searches. If you do those things and you are the first person to invent the great idea, you can prove you are the owner of the worldwide intellectual property rights to your great idea! Congratulations! You can sleep easy now! You can also take time to determine if you want to protect your great idea even further. That is to say, these steps help you stake a claim to your great idea, but you must remember that you have not yet protected the invention by way of a patent. Just what is so good about a patent anyway? Let's find out!

Maximum Protection for Your Great Idea for an Invention

My client sat in front of me and told me that he did not have a lot of money and he was making his house payments with his credit card, but that he really thought his idea was a good one and he wanted to know what I thought. (I thought he was nuts!) I told him that several things concerned me. The first thing that concerned me was his great idea. He had just explained that the state of the art for replacing a car window was either to take a hammer and knock it out or take a big knife and cut it out. The first way was messy and the second way always damaged the frame of the car. His great idea was a saw with a reciprocating blade that was covered by a sheath so that you could cut the window out neatly without damage to the frame. I told him that the concern I had was that his invention was a saw, and, you know, there are plenty of saws around. Next, I was concerned because there was no guarantee that a patent would issue just because he filed an application. Then I told him even if you get a patent, there is no guarantee that it will help you make any money; the product has to be marketable for the patent to help. Finally, I said, "And, you're making your house payments with a credit card!"

Well, he insisted, and we filed the application, and the patent issued. We were having lunch a year or so later, and I asked him, "So, how's the saw thingy going for you?" And he said, "Good. Sold $100,000 worth of 'em." And I said, "You're kidding. You sold $100,000 worth of those things last year?" And he said, "No, last month." What a country! He sold the pants off his saw. He made an international business out of it! How great is that!

That client taught me that I am no predictor as to whether or not your great idea is worth filing a patent application for. You must decide that. I also learned that if you don't believe in your great idea, no one else will either, including maybe even your patent attorney!

The Good News About Getting a Patent for Your Great Idea

A patent is a monopoly! (Patent attorneys all over the world are aghast that one of the brethren has broken ranks and uttered the "M" word. I have spent countless hours listening to very smart lawyers explain why a patent isn't a true monopoly, but I am still not so sure.) Anyway, for real people, a monopoly is a perfect description of what you get when you get a patent. You get the exclusive right to stop people from making, using, or selling your patented thing for the life of the patent. Hmmm, sounds pretty much like a monopoly to me!

The way it goes is like this: A patent is a something-less-than-20-year right that the federal government gives inventors. When I started practicing to be a patent attorney (way back before there were "intellectual property" lawyers), a patent lasted 17 years from the date it issued, no matter how long the bureaucrats in Washington took. However, in the interest of "harmonization," a patent now lasts 20 years from the date you file it. Say what? Yep, because you don't have a patent when you file, but only a patent application, you have absolutely no idea how long your patent will last when you file the application! If the patent office takes ten years to issue the patent, it lasts ten years. Ouch! They sold this cheesy "harmonization" to the little guys (remember, the big guys don't care because they have all the money) by pointing out that the average time it took to get a patent back then was 18 months. This was a good deal for the little guy, they said, because it meant that patents on average would now last 18½ years. Can you guess what has happened since? Yep, in my experience, it is taking longer and longer to get a patent. Until it takes three years I guess no one will complain too much. If that ever happens, my thought is that it will be the perfect time to de-harmonize our system and go back to the old "17 years from issue" deal.

Note too that only the "inventor" can file the patent application. This is important. It is illegal for any person to whom you show your great idea to file a patent application on it because he or she did not invent it! That is not inventing, that's stealing. This is true whether you showed the person your great idea in confidence or at a cocktail party. This also means that you can't add your mom as an inventor just because you love her, and you can't keep her off if she actually invented the anti-gravity device. Now, I am sure that in the course of human history someone's neighbor has peeked over the fence and filed a patent application on something he saw but did not invent. Still, assuming that the other person could prove he invented it (a signed witnessed document sounds like a good idea), he would prevail against the person who committed "fraud on the Patent Office."

Fraud on the Patent Office is pretty cool if you are the person proving it. If you can prove that someone filed the application claiming to be the inventor but wasn't, the patent is thrown out! You don't even have to worry about them proving that you copied the actual great idea for the invention. In the case where you are accused of infringing someone's patent and you can show "fraud on the Patent Office," you win even if you copied the thing exactly! Sometimes, for example, you see a company that has a research and development lab, and every patent has the name of the head of R&D as an inventor. Unless it is a one-man shop, it is a good place to start looking to see if his name was added just because he's the boss and not because he actually ever invented anything.

Also, patents are federal only; there are no state patents. The great state of Texas, however, in its short history as the Republic of Texas, actually did have a patent office. It issued patents for useful things like a brick-making machine, a lamp, and a shingle machine. Other countries have their own patent systems too.

The Bad News About Getting a Patent for Your Great Idea: Three Tests

So the good news is that if you get a patent, you get a limited monopoly for a short period of time. The bad news is they don't just give away patents for great ideas. Every great idea, including yours, must pass three tests before a patent will be granted.

The First Test: Useful

The first test is that your great idea must be "useful." In my entire career I have never had to tell a single client, "Hit the road. That great idea is not even useful as a paperweight!" In fact, the first test involves a very low threshold. I mean, even a lump of lead is useful as a paperweight! Any useful purpose will do. It does not have to be high science or complicated. The "Rubik's Cube" puzzle, for example, was patented!

The Second Test: New

The second test is not much more difficult to pass, and that is that your great idea must be "new." By that they essentially mean that so long as the identical thing has not been done before, it is "new" under the patent system. Well, I am here to tell you that no one has ever asked me to apply for a patent on some great idea of theirs that they just bought at WAL-MART. Here is where the old saying "Necessity is the mother of invention" comes in. What usually happens is that the inventor was minding his or her own business trying to make a living, when they needed something to help them with what they were doing. The first place they looked was WAL-MART, K-MART, AUTO MART, or one of the other "Marts," and they found nothing. That should have been their first inkling that they might have a great idea. Then they dug around a little or a lot more and did a "layperson's" (lawyer code for "not a lawyer") "search of the relevant art" (think patent and literature search in the field of the invention), and then they came to see me. If I have seen the identical thing somewhere, I will tell them; but usually I tell them, "It's new to me too!"

Great googly moogly, you are two-thirds of the way home to getting a patent! But wait. Now comes the hard part: the third test.

The Third Test: Not Obvious

The third test is where the rubber meets the road in the patent world. In addition to being useful and new, every great idea that has ever been patented has also been…(Are you ready for this? No, you're not, but here goes…) "a non-obvious improvement on a pre-existing device." Usually, my clients who have not fallen asleep by this time raise both eyebrows and say, "Huh?" Here again, the law is not particularly clear or seemingly logical. Here is what the third test means. What you do is create a "hypothetical" person of "ordinary" skill in the art, and you pose the problem that you have solved to this hypothetical person. This hypothetical person is a person of ordinary skill in the field, not a genius but not a slug either. In patent litigation you sometimes spend a lot of time identifying what "ordinary" means. My thought is if you are talking about the art of nuclear reactors, it is a Ph.D. in nuclear reactors with lots of on-the-job training. If the art is surf boarding, it may be some high school surfer.

Anyway, this person of ordinary skill is presumed to know all the patents that have ever been issued in this field and to read popular reactor/surfer magazines. If the hypothetical person can solve the problem you solved, the way you did, in ignorance of your solution, then your great idea is an ordinary design choice that anyone of ordinary skill in the art would think of, and is *not* patentable. If, however, the hypothetical person of ordinary skill in the art cannot solve the problem the way you did in ignorance of your great idea, then your great idea is a non-obvious improvement on pre-existing technology, and *is* patentable.

A friendly aside: You should instinctively know to hide your wallet whenever lawyers start talking about "hypothetical people" as the legal test for anything. I mean, who's to say whether my hypothetical guy is smarter or dumber than your hypothetical guy? We could argue that until the end of time! Anyway, the third test is the hard test, and the truth is that everything is obvious once you know how it's done. A paper clip is pretty darned obvious once you've seen one, isn't it? Sure it is. If all the paper clip companies suddenly went out of business, I bet you could probably work up a prototype and get going right away. But that's not the test. The test, prior to the known existence of paper clips, is to not look at a paper clip and decide if it is obvious. The test is: Solve this problem:

How do you join paper together without punching holes in it? And the hypothetical guy of ordinary skill in the art, someone working in an office, perhaps, knows all the patents that have been issued in the paper joining field and he reads *Popular Paper Joining Monthly,* and if the best solutions he can come up with are string and rocks and glue, well then, the "removably attachable, nondeforming attachment means" (which is how some patent attorney might describe a paper clip) is a non-obvious improvement and patentable!

Patent attorneys who "prosecute" (lawyer code for "prepare and file") patent applications spend a lot of their time (and, therefore, their clients' money) arguing this third test with the patent office. Given the limited time the patent examiners have to examine the applications, I believe they do a great job. But again, every thing is obvious when you know how, and the examiner cannot actually apply the third test because they have just read your solution to the problem! They are not ignorant of the solution; they know exactly how you did it. It is just like the Heisenberg uncertainty principle you learned about in high school. Heisenberg said you can't accurately measure something because the act of measuring it alters the thing being measured. (I think he is probably correct with small, atomic-sized things but wrong when one is measuring elephants!) Anyway, the patent examiner will read your application, look at your drawings, and then send you a "First Office Action," which details his or her analysis of your application. (More on this later.) One thing to keep in mind is that the patent examiner who reviews your application has probably done the equivalent of millions of dollars of patent searches in the relevant art, and you can be sure there is some art they know about that you and/or your attorney do not. For now, just don't be surprised when they show you art you never dreamed existed.

Everything Ever Invented Is a Combination of Old Stuff

One other thing to do if you are thinking that your great idea may not be patentable because all you did is take part A from RADIO SHACK and combine it with part B from TOYS-R-US is this: Stop thinking that! Everything that has ever been invented is a combination of old stuff. Unless the Martians land and give us some new goo, we are stuck with a finite list of ingredients. This does not mean, however, that there is any end in sight for new inventions and great ideas. A commissioner for Patents in the 1800s, when asked by Congress to justify the existence of the U.S. Patent Office, couldn't do it and said that every thing that could be invented had already been invented, and you could just go ahead and close up the place! This was before POST-ITS, for crying out loud! The problem the commissioner had was a common one, though. It is the belief that because there is a limited, although large, list of ingredients, surely someday we will have invented everything that ever could be invented. Wrong! That computer between your ears has an infinite number of great ideas left! And the truth is, again, everything that has ever been invented and patented is a combination of old stuff!

A Patent Is Not a Money Tree or a Gun

There is some more bad news about patents. A patent is not a money tree or a gun! Sorry, just getting a patent does not mean you can force people to give you their money. Only if they want to make, use, or sell your great idea for an invention does the patent make sense. Then a patent can be a money tree. The University of Florida, for example, has pulled more than $80 million off the money tree from their patent for salty lemonade! Still, not every great idea that is patented is a money tree. Most, in fact, do not even grow into a shrub big enough to pay for the patent. Ouch! On the other hand, a patent is not a gamble like the one you take when you buy a lottery ticket. Not even close. If you have done what I suggest and you know what the market is, you know the cost-benefit of your investment and what effect a patent would have on your return. Then the investment in a patent will be just that, an investment and not a pure gamble.

A Patent Is a Two-Edged Sword

Even more bad news: A patent is a two-edged sword. If you get a patent, you must be prepared to defend it. A patent is a powerful weapon you can use to keep your competitors away from your great idea, but only if they respect your ability to use your weapon. Some companies may agree to a license and start paying you money right away. Some you might have to work harder to convince. Some companies, in fact, have a policy of "copy everything and let them sue us if we did anything wrong." This kind of arrogance is all around us and is a modern-day expression of the old saying "might makes right." I also think this attitude is a function of the fact that business entities—corporations that exist in their own right long after the founder dies, is fired, or has been sent to jail—have no soul. There is no human to whom you can go who has the power to say, "You know, you are right. Your patent is valid and we will pay you a fair royalty starting today!" Instead, you are told, "Our lawyers will talk to your lawyers." So the point is, be prepared to defend your patent by suing individuals or corporations who infringe it, or else do not waste your time and money getting it. (Patent litigation, by the way, is the most profitable thing patent attorneys can do. Many law firms actually lose money on the patent applications they prepare and file in the hope of getting the lucrative litigation case. One common estimate for the cost of a patent litigation case, always spoken in hushed, reverent tones, is *$1 million on each side!* Are you beginning to see why the big guys have all the lawyers and no one wants to mess with the little guys?)

What Goes into a Patent Application?

As we discussed above, you have two options when considering a patent for your great idea: You can start with a patent search, or skip it and go right ahead with a patent application. There is no law that requires you to do a patent search before you file a patent application, so you can just start with an application! As a practical matter, that is the only way you will ever know for sure whether or not your great idea is patentable. After all, it is the Patent Office that has the power to say yes or no that determines if you get a patent, not any patent attorney! The problem is that patent applications cost more than searches, as we will discuss later on. How much a patent application does cost is, in fact, the number one question I am asked. I understand why it is asked so much: Money does matter to real people. The problem is that it is pretty much like asking a car dealer what a car costs. He will look at you and ask, what brand? A Lexus is one thing, and a Kia is another. So no patent attorney can tell you what the cost of the application will be until he or she knows what your great idea is. At that point, they can tell you. What they tell you depends on what kind of businessperson they are. Some lawyers do fixed fees, some do estimated fees, and some do contingent fees. Whatever type of fee they quote you, don't agree to it until you understand what it does and does not include. My thought is, again, if you don't understand something don't sign it!

Here is what I do. I treat my clients like I like to be treated when I drive my big old Suburban in to get an oil change. "How much to change the oil?" "Fifty bucks." "OK." Then, when I get a bill for $57.95, I say, OK. But if the bill is $557, I say, no way! The point is that it is an estimate and may be a little more or less, but it won't be way off. I hope to send shockingly big bills to my clients, but they will never get a big bill that is a shocking surprise!

A Patent Application Is an Enabling Document

Whatever the invention, and whatever the estimate, you need to know what the patent attorney is doing for his or her fees. Basically, the inventor has the obligation to submit an enabling document such that a person of ordinary skill in the art can, if the application issues as a patent, read and understand and practice the invention. So you have to tell a story that has never been told before about something that has never existed before. A patent application is, therefore, not just a fill-in-the-blank exercise. You have to tell them what the problem is that you have solved, how other people have tried to solve the problem up to now so far as you know, and what you have done that is so cool. You then give them a detailed explanation of your invention with reference to drawings showing how it goes together and how it works. The drawings are not mechanical drawings to be used to make the thing, but rather instructional figures to aid the reader in understanding how your great idea works.

The Key to a Patent Are the Claims

In any event, the creation of the story takes time, but where the patent attorney spends most of his or her time (and most of his client's money) at this stage of the process is in the preparation of the "claims." These are the most difficult part to draft and the most important part of the patent application and of any patent that issues. They are what you get when you get a patent! When you get a patent, you get the right to stop people from making, using, and selling what? What is set forth in your claims! You don't get the right to stop people from selling any old anti-gravity device. You get only the right to stop them from selling the anti-gravity device as set forth in your claims. The claims, if you have ever read a patent, are those weird numbered paragraphs at the end of the story/patent that are usually in the form of almost totally unintelligible lawyer gibberish, and which most people rightly refuse to read for fear of losing their sanity.

Unfortunately, claims are, again, really important, so inventors of great ideas ought to know something about them. Here's what you should know about claims. They are analogous to the "meets and bounds" descriptions for pieces of real property. Each piece of dirt A is separate from another piece of dirt B according to the deed. You know when your neighbor's dog is in your yard, for example. Well, the patent attorney's job is to draft the claims to your invention as broadly as he or she can with a straight face. The attorney is not going to leave any of your great idea on the table, so to speak.

"Broad" Claims Are Very Important

But what does "broadly" mean? This is really, really important. Some patent attorneys have said that they can get a patent on anything. This is not as outrageous as it may sound. What that means is that for any invention they can draft a claim that is so narrow that the patent office will allow it. But is that any good for you? I suppose it depends on whether you want a piece of paper that is valuable only as a wall hanging or if you want meaningful protection. I will say that what most real people want is broad protection for their great idea, not some academic exercise that is not worth the paper it is printed on.

Here is how I think of the terms "broad" and "narrow" when it comes to claims. A broad claim for the place I live is "the Universe." That includes everything! A narrow claim for the place I live is "the Universe, planet Earth, North America, the United States of America, Florida, Santa Rosa County, Gulf Breeze, 913 Gulf Breeze Parkway, Suite 43, this brown, wooden, hurricane-ravaged desk." That is pretty darn narrow. You can be standing in my office, and if you are not at my desk, you do not infringe that narrow claim. So, in general, broad claims = good, narrow claims = bad. However, never forget the commercial side. If everybody wants your very narrow improvement, then even a very narrow claim will do!

A Sad Story of Narrow Claims

This reminds me of a sad story. I had a new client come in the other day that wanted to hire me to sue a very big company for patent infringement. The client had formed a company, raised money, and was ready to sell the product to the very big company but then discovered that the very big company was making the exact same product without the client's help. He was, to put it mildly, hot. The key to his case, of course, was the patent. Well, it turns out the patent had been prepared by the inventor, who was sitting right in front of me and who was a part of the group. He had worked for a big company in the past and was proud to tell me that he had many patents in his name. He had been through the process so many times that he had decided to save the money on a patent attorney and to prepare and file the application himself, and he had gotten a patent! That's the good news. The sad news is that as I looked at the claims that he had written and that were the basis of his patent, it was clear he did not understand that the claims defined the scope of his patent. I had to advise him that although the very big company was indeed taking the guts of his idea and copying it exactly, they were not infringing any of his very narrow claims. Ouch! There were some options available, but none were as strong as broad claims for his great idea would have been.

What Does "Patent Pending" Mean?

When it comes to drafting a patent application, what most patent attorneys do (I really don't know what they do, but this is the way I do it and it makes sense to me, and I really don't know how you could draft a patent application that makes sense any other way) is to come to an understanding of the invention and then draft the claims. Once the claims are drafted, the attorney prepares the rest of the application so that the entire application reflects the claims. After the draft application, including rough figures, is prepared, the client gets to take a whack at it with his or her red pen. Thereafter the lawyer amends the application to include the appropriate changes and then finalizes the application for filing. The inventor reads it one last time, and signs the declaration of inventorship and other forms as needed, and it is sent off to the U.S. Patent Office. The instant it is received in the Patent Office, your great idea is "patent pending." That just sounds so cool, doesn't it? You see it everywhere on things. But what does it mean?

"Patent pending" simply means you have filed a patent application, nothing more or less. You can't say it if it isn't true, although some ad companies seem to think it's OK because it adds a certain panache. Wrong! If you haven't filed an application, you cannot say "patent pending." And just because you are "patent pending" doesn't mean your competitors can't copy your great idea exactly! They can, and there is nothing illegal about doing that. Remember, you have the right to stop people from making, using, and selling your great idea only *after* you get a patent. Also, if and when you do get a patent, you can't go back and make your competitors pay you for the copying they did while you were "patent pending." Not too strong, is it?

About the best thing I have been able to say about the benefit of being "patent pending" is that it raises the price of playing poker! The competitors don't know when you filed, unless you agree to let the Patent Office publish your application 18 months after you file (more on that later), and they don't know what your claims are even though they can examine your product. So they don't know if you filed one year or one minute ago, and they don't know how broad your claims may be. As a result, they may decide to copy something else that doesn't say "patent pending."

Also, if your competitors decide to copy your patent-pending great idea, the best way to think of it is that they are spending advertising dollars you won't have to spend and generating a client base bigger than you alone could have generated. And when your patent finally does issue, all those clients your competitor stirred up must come to you!

What Types of Patent Applications Are There?

You might be surprised to know that there are four types of patent applications but only three types of patents! The three types of patents are utility patents, design patents, and plant patents. A utility patent is what most people think of when they talk about patents; it covers functional great ideas like anti-gravity devices, better mousetraps, and so forth. (In the interest of full disclosure, I missed this question in my law school class. How embarrassing!) Utility patents are granted for processes, machines, articles of manufacture, and compositions of matter that are useful, novel, and non-obvious improvements over the prior art. Design patents are granted for novel and non-obvious ornamental designs for articles of manufacture. Plant patents are granted for certain asexually reproduced plants.

Even though there are only three types of patents, there are four types of applications: one for each of the three types of patents and one relatively new type called a "provisional application." This type of application is everything a "real" utility application is except it has no claims! Now the careful reader knows that the key to a patent application, and what you get if you get a patent, is set forth in the claims. What possible purpose, therefore, could the provisional patent application serve? That is a very good question, because in the United States there is no need to rush to file a patent application, as there is in every other country in the world, because we use the "first to invent" rule, not the "first to file" rule. So in the United States, simply make a written record of your great idea and get it witnessed, and you don't have to file anything in a hurry, including a provisional application.

There is one real-world situation that could warrant filing a provisional application. Let's say you are going to present your great idea at a conference in Hawaii next week. (Be sure to take your patent attorney with you on those trips, by the way! Never forget your patent attorney!) You don't have time to have a proper non-provisional application prepared and filed, but you could prepare and file a provisional. If you do, the filing of a provisional application allows you to say "patent pending," and you have one year from the filing of the provisional to file a non-provisional application that relates back to it. Plus, the filing of the non-provisional before you make your great idea public gives you a year from the filing of the provisional within which to start the process of filing foreign patent applications. (More about foreign patents soon!) Remember, everywhere else in the world, you must spend the money on a patent application before you introduce your great idea to the public. (The cynical side of me thinks that the provisional application is just a way to get Americans used to the idea of filing hurry-up applications so that "they" can "harmonize" our laws completely with those of the rest of the world by making the United States a "first to file" country too. This is a bad idea for the little guy, in my opinion. In fact, I bet that if the little guys in the rest of the world had a vote, they would choose to harmonize their cheesy systems with the way we do it in the States!)

How Long Does the Patent Process Take?

Speaking of the benefits of harmonization, remember that they "harmonized" the U.S. system to enable our patents to last 20 years from filing instead of 17 years from issuance. Back then statistics showed that, on average, it took 18 months for a patent to work itself out of the system. Thus, we were told, on average, this would be a good deal for U.S. inventors, giving the average patent a life of 18½ years. Well, in my experience, ever since they harmonized the life of a patent, it has taken longer and longer to get the First Office Action I talked about. Just this year I had a First Office Action mailed more than three years after the application was filed. It seems to me things are slipping. Still, in fairness to the U.S. Patent Office, they do review the length of the examination process and add time to the life of the patent when the delay is deemed too much. (I still like the old way, where you knew for sure how long your patent would last no matter what the bureaucrats did or how long they took doing it.)

After a Long Wait, Expect Rejection!

In any event, after spending the money on a patent application and getting your great idea "patent pending," be prepared to wait a good long time. A year, year and a half, or two years is not uncommon these days. Then, when you finally do get the First Office Action from the patent examiner assigned to your invention, most of the time it is a First Office Action *rejection*! I can hear you now: "You have got to be kidding. I spend a lot of money to file this patent application, I wait forever to hear from them, and the first thing they tell me is no?" Yes. That is the bad news. The good news is, they can't say, "No, and guess why!" The patent examiner must tell you why they rejected the application and give you the references they used to support the rejection. (They used to send you copies of the patents or other art they cited, but now you have to go online and find it yourself.) Anyway, what, you might ask, is wrong with this picture? Is the Patent Office messed up or are patent attorneys? Neither. Both are just doing their jobs. Remember, your patent attorney's job is to claim your invention as broadly as possible. The Patent Office's job is to issue patents that aren't so broad that they trespass on someone else's pre-existing property. Even if you spent a lot of money on a search, you can see that you don't have to be a patent examiner very long in order to perform effectively millions and millions of dollars of searches. So the examiner reads the application, looks at the drawings, and focuses on the claims. Then the examiner sends the rejection for the application, saying which claims are too broad and why.

Three Things the Rejection Can Mean

At that point, the rejection can mean one of three things. First, the examiner may be right! Sometimes, unbeknownst to you, the exact same invention has been devised before, and you are dead! Second, the examiner may rightly claim that some of your idea has been done before, but your great idea may be granted a patent if you narrow your claims a little. Last, the examiner could be wrong! In that case, you can explain the invention to the examiner and point out where the error in the analysis is, and the great invention could be granted a patent as applied for.

By far the most common occurrence is the second one. This requires the inventor to review the Office Action and the references and work with the attorney to carve out the largest remaining parts of the great idea for the patent. This is done by filing an "amendment" in which the claims are amended to more narrowly define the invention. The claims can be amended or rewritten altogether if need be, but one rule you need to know is that once the application is submitted, you cannot add any new information. Saying, "I forgot this important part of the invention and want to add it now" will fall on stone-deaf ears. This partly explains why patents read so funny to folks. The patent attorney's job is to explain the invention in a variety of ways, to look at it from various angles if you will, because you never know when some little part will become the key to getting the patent.

Appeals Are More Common Today

Most of the time, the issues can be worked out between the inventor and the examiner. But sometimes you may believe you are right while the examiner feels he or she is right, and you can't work it out. In that case, the inventor can appeal the examiner's decision to the Board of Patent Appeals. In the first 20 years of my practice, I filed two appeals. In the last six years I have filed a half-dozen or more. In general, I have won the appeal when I thought I should have, and I have been mostly pleased with the system. I have wondered why it seems necessary to appeal the examiner's decision more often now than in the past. I do not know the true reason, but I have had an examiner tell me that because of the public outcry over the AMAZON.com "one click" patent (U.S. Patent 5,960,411), he is refusing to grant patents for inventions now for which he would have in the past. He explained that examiners who grant a patent for an invention that, upon internal review, is deemed not to have been allowable will get a negative letter in their files. Two negatives, and the examiner is looking for a new job. But if it is found on appeal that the examiner should have granted the patent but didn't, he gets no negative letter. Sounds like a bureaucratic possibility to me.

In case you don't know about the "one click" situation, a patent was issued for a system of ordering things on the Internet by clicking only once. Everyone in the Internet world went nuts. "Are you crazy?" they said "That is so old; everyone has been doing that for years! The Patent Office must be going nuts!" Well, my thought is, if it truly is old, then prove it. That's all you have to do to defeat any patent. Show the judge or jury a 1945 copy of *Popular Science* magazine showing the exact same anti-gravity device, and the patent is gone! It is not the fault of the U.S. Patent Office that occasionally some patents issue that shouldn't. They do a very good job, the best in the world, but they are not perfect. So I hope the reason you might run into an appeal if you file a patent application doesn't involve undue pressure on the examiners, although, for whatever reason, this is a greater possibility now, in my experience, than in the past.

Interested in Foreign Patents? Think "Sailboat"

You know what a sailboat is, don't you? It is a great big black hole into which you throw an inordinate amount of money for very little return! I have known people who have owned sailboats but could not find anybody to go sailing with them. Even their own families soon found that the thrill of sailing was far outweighed by just about anything else they could think of to do—clean their rooms, shine their shoes, mow the dog, wash the yard—anything at all! They say the two best days for a sailboat owner are the day he buys the boat and the day he sells it. Keep this in mind when you start thinking about foreign patents!

In my mind, foreign patents make sense if the product is a cash cow of Alaskan proportions and you actually have a business in the foreign country in which you wish to file. Otherwise, if you have never been to Zimbabwe, how do you know if they are ignoring your patent there or not? In general, in my experience, foreign patents make sense for the big guys but not the little guys, at least not for the first great idea. Foreign patents are very expensive and hard to enforce, and that should be all you need to know about them. For the little guy, my thinking is to focus on protecting the great idea in the greatest market in the world, the United States, and think about foreign patents when the first great idea generates a surplus of funds to devote to your second great idea. And this I do know about inventors: They have the gift of invention, and that gift is also a curse. The curse is that they are going to have to die for them to quit noodling around with the first invention, and they are seriously at risk for having a second great idea too!

One of the main reasons people think they need a foreign patent is to protect themselves in the countries that specialize in making knock-offs of the originals. The countries in which the illegal copies are made are typically those countries that have no regard for laws in general, much less intellectual property laws. Think communist dictatorships. Unless you are related to the dictator or have all the money in the world to pay for the privilege of having your patent selected for protection, it is, in my opinion, a waste of time to get patents in these countries. Your focus should not be on where are you going to get ripped off, but where you are going to sell the great idea. That's where you need patent protection!

Time and Cost

Time, tide and noon meal formation wait for no man! We used to say this a lot at the Naval Academy, usually when we were late for noon meal formation. But if you are in a hurry to protect your great idea with a patent, you are messing with the wrong system. Patent applications take a good long time. Two to three years is pretty normal. There is a process to expedite certain great ideas that may have particular benefits to society—energy-saving anti-gravity devices, for example. However, even this process is slow. I have waited a year to get approval of a request to expedite an application! So having a good sense of the commercial life of your great idea is often helpful in making the decision about whether or not to file for a patent. If the shelf life of the great idea is six months, forget about a patent!

What does it cost to buy a car/patent? If you answered, "It depends," congratulations, you have just finished the first year of law school-speak! Obviously, the great idea governs what the cost of the application will be. Simple ideas generally mean lower costs. In the course of the last year the cost of the applications I have filed has run anywhere from, say, $3,500 to $9,500, and none of them have been exceedingly complex ideas. The most expensive application I have ever filed was about $20,000. (This is probably amusing to some of my fellow patent attorneys; I am sure there are patent attorneys somewhere who charge more than $20,000 for the simplest thing they deal with!) Anyway, when it comes time for you to know what the cost would be to file a patent application for your great idea, ask your patent attorney for an estimate. The estimate should include the lawyer's fees and the government filing fees and all other costs, such as drawing fees, assignments, and anything else you will be charged for. It should also set out when the fees are due and if any retainer you give the lawyer is "refundable" or not. I take a retainer consisting of a portion of the total fee, with the balance due upon approval of the application by the client. The retainer is refundable until I earn it. It just covers me against the risk of doing work and not getting paid for it. (You might be shocked to know that, when I was much younger, I would draft the application and send it to the client with a bill, and sometimes I wouldn't ever hear from that client again. Hmmm.)

Well, now you have the information you need to decide how to proceed to protect your great idea for an invention. The basic and most important steps to take to protect your great idea are free. So *take them first*! Then, if a patent is warranted, hire a competent patent attorney to prepare and file the patent application and assist you during and after the process. Of all the areas of intellectual property law, patent law is the most complicated, and it is the area where you are most likely to need, and benefit from, the services of a lawyer. Sorry about that!

4

Free Protection for Your Great Creative Work

$\mathbf{M}$any of the most valuable ideas that people create are not new ideas at all. Rather, they are magnificent expressions of an already existing idea! This chapter will discuss what these types of great ideas look like and how to decide which ideas rise to the level of a protectable expression.

What Types of Creative Great Ideas Are Protectable?

Everything you need to know about protecting your original works of art and authorship that you haven't protected any other way, you learned when you learned about plagiarism in high school. There you learned that it is very bad behavior to copy the other guy's stuff; it's plagiarism, it's stealing, don't do it or it will go on your permanent record! Not only is it bad behavior in academic circles, but it is against the law to copy someone else's original works of art or authorship. What law is it against? Copyright law! Copyright law is a very narrow form of protection in that it protects only original expressions of an idea, and not the idea itself. Anyone can write a book about the Civil War in America, but you cannot copy *Gone With the Wind*.

Well, if all you get is protection for your expression of an idea, is it worth very much? You tell me. Let's say I am inspired to paint a picture of sunflowers in a vase. The same subject painted by Van Gogh is worth considerably more than my version, I can tell you that for sure.

Nevin's Theory on Why Bill Gates Is the Richest Man on the Planet

Need another example of the value of copyrights? How about Nevin's theory on why Bill Gates is the richest man on the planet. Because I have not confirmed this with Mr. Gates, I offer this as my theory only. It goes like this. *Fact:* Bill Gates had a business—measuring traffic flow, among other things—when he responded to an IBM request to submit an operating system for the company to test. *Fact:* IBM paid Bill about $180,000, and he created the operating system and sent it to IBM. *Fact:* IBM selected Bill's operating system over all the others. *Fact:* Without a written assignment of copyright to IBM, IBM got only the right to use the operating system on IBM computers and Bill got to sell his operating system to the rest of the world because, as an "independent contractor," Bill owned the copyrights! *Theory:* IBM was rushing their "PC" to the market to compete with this goofy company called Apple (like there would ever be a time when people would have personal computers in their homes; get real), knowing that the value of the machine was the hardware, not this software stuff, so ownership of the copyright to the software was a non-issue! Sounds right to me, and fits copyright law perfectly!

As we have already discussed, even though independent contractors are paid to create original works of art and/or authorship, the independent contractor owns the copyrights according to copyright law, *not* the person who paid for it. The only way the person who paid for the original work of art to own it is to be assigned the copyrights in writing by the independent contractor! On the other hand, had IBM, for example, had one of its many software writers create the operating system for its PCs, Mr. Gates would have had to find another way to become the richest man on the planet. Copyright law says that when the employee of a company creates an original work of art or authorship, the company owns the copyrights because it is considered a "work for hire." Go figure!

OK, so now that we have reviewed the ownership issues, what kinds of original things are we talking about? We are talking about wonderfully great ideas, the kinds of great ideas that define your life: your favorite song, software program, book, movie, poem, video game, painting, play, musical, and sculpture, to name just a few. The very fabric of people's lives. We consider the people who create such expressions of their great ideas artists and authors! And they should consider themselves intellectual property owners of precious inheritable property! So long as it is *original*! Remember, you get no rights from copying other people's stuff. (And just because it is easy to copy things today, that doesn't make it right!)

What Great Ideas Do Not Qualify for Copyright Protection?

Not everything you come up with is protectable by copyright. Works that consist entirely of common information or matters of common knowledge are not protectable by copyright. For example, standard calendars and the common markings on rulers or measuring tapes lack the requisite originality or authorship. I have often had clients ask me how to protect their new idea for a bumper sticker. The short answer is, you can't! Not by a patent, or a trademark or copyrights! There is just not enough there to protect in any way. The key to bumper stickers is to get there first and sell them fast! You might see a copyright notice on a bumper sticker, but it would cover only any original art work on it, and not the words, if it covered anything at all. Remember, lots of people don't know the rules, and they may put the copyright notice or "patent pending" on their product just because it sounds good!

Likewise, there is no copyright protection for a single word, method, system process, fact, or history! Furthermore, ideas, concepts, or procedures alone are not considered works of authorship and cannot be protected by copyright. Remember, only the expression of an idea is protectable, not the idea itself!

What Is a Copyright?

You hear the term "copyright" a lot, but what sort of right is it? A copyright is a form of intellectual property right granted by the federal government for "original works of authorship." And a copyright is actually more than just one right. The copyright itself includes five basic rights regarding the use or exploitation of the copyrighted work. With certain limitations, the owner of a copyright has the exclusive right to (1) reproduce the copyrighted work, (2) prepare derivative works, (3) distribute copies, (4) perform the copyrighted work publicly, and (5) display the copyrighted work publicly. The most basic right, the one most people associate with copyrights, is the right to stop other people from making copies. There is no question that this is an important, primary right, but the right to prevent the creation of derivative works is not far behind. Think "Ice Age Two." Once the rights to the original are established, the copyright owner (you) can prevent others from making derivatives of the original, which can be worth more than the original in some cases!

What Is the Value of a Copyright?

You might be asking yourself, if a copyright is so easy to get, what good is it? Well, a copyright prevents others from benefiting unfairly from the author's creativity. The value of the copyright is in requiring that others either make their own investment of time, money, and creativity to create their own expression of your great idea, or else purchase the rights to use the author's work. You can't stop someone else from creating software for games, but you can stop them from copying yours!

Two Cases with Different Results

The most difficult part of copyright law is understanding that the "idea" is *not* protectable. Once the idea for a book about places to scuba dive, for example, is made public, anybody can be inspired to write a book about scuba diving. They just can't copy yours or make non-substantial changes in yours. The question is, is there a substantial similarity in the protectable parts of the book between yours and theirs? Facts aren't protectable. A simple list of dive sites on the California coast is not protectable. A detailed description of what a trip up the coast from south to north was like and what you encountered at each site, along with your personal experiences and advice, is highly protectable. For such a book, simply listing the dive sites in reverse order from north to south and reprinting the book is not permissible and will result in a judgment of copyright infringement against the copier. (I know because I handled just this case for an author and won!)

Most infringers will attempt to focus the discussion on the differences between the copy and the original. I once had the uncomfortable occasion of defending a claim of infringement of an apartment locator booklet. My advice had been to settle because the similarities were significant, but my client wanted his "day in court." Since he was paying, I said, "OK, but you won't like it much!" During his much-anticipated day in court my client had just finished a half-hour explanation of how his booklet was different from the other guy's booklet, when the judge held up the two booklets side by side, showing that they aligned almost perfectly, and asked me to explain the differences! I allowed it since I had nothing to add to my client's testimony, and in the recess called by the judge my client decided to settle! (Not a fun day for the client, but at least the lawyer got paid.) Again, when it comes to determining whether the works are too close, it is not the differences that matter but the similarities!

What Are "Moral Rights?"

"Moral rights" are a special form of copyright protection that exists only for works of visual art. When an artist paints a mural on a building, his moral rights attach to the artwork even if he actually sells the copyrights to the art. His moral rights allow him to prevent even the copyright owner from destroying, damaging, or changing the artwork. The primary authority for moral rights in the United States is the Visual Artists Rights Act of 1990. Moral rights have a greater scope in other countries in that they cover other types of copyrightable things. In the United States, the artist's moral rights may not be transferred or end upon the artist's death. Just as copyrights may be transferred in writing, moral rights may be waived if done so in writing too.

What Is the "Public Domain?"

As the Copyright Office Web site patiently explains, the "public domain" is not a place! It is what happens to works of art and authorship after the copyright expires. Once a copyright expires, anyone is free to copy the previously protected thing! This explains why Disney was in such a frantic state to help ensure that the copyright term was extended recently!

Many wonderful works are in the public domain, such as the movie *It's a Wonderful Life*. This explains why, in addition to being a great movie, it is seen so much on TV! When it comes to using things that are in the public domain, there is no limit. It is the perfect thing to use in your own work of art or authorship because no permission to use it is required. The trick is to make absolutely sure that something is in fact in the public domain before using any of it.

How Do You Know If Something Is in the Public Domain?

If in doubt, ask! Generally, because most authors and artists know to put their copyright notice on their works, your first clue that something might not be in the public domain is a copyright notice with the year 2006! Often you see a current copyright notice on something you know for sure is in the public domain, like the Bible. What's up with that? In such a case, it is not the public domain work that is covered, but only the original analysis or new introduction or whatever else has been added to the work. Again, if in doubt, ask! I know asking is hard to do and often results in a rejection. But this is, in my opinion, better than a lawsuit! If someone has the copyright on some work you want to use and they will not grant you permission to use it, *don't*! A good business rule is, always get permission before using any copyrighted thing. Better yet, always get *written* permission from whoever controls the work, or don't use it at all!

As I was writing the book, I looked at the picture in Figure 4.1 hanging on my wall and knew it had been drawn for my friend John Sullivan by a friend of his. John and I had started a novelty business selling coffee cups with the image on them to lawyers. Thankfully, we did not quit our day jobs! Anyway, I was sure the copyright had been assigned to us and if not that John's friend would

Figure 4.1. "Billable owls."

give me permission to use the picture in the book. When I couldn't find the copyright assignment, I called John to confirm that his friend would OK this. However, he said he remembered that a friend of mine had drawn it! So I took the picture off the wall and examined it and noticed it had the date it was drawn, January 10, 1985, but no copyright notice! Thus, the good news is even though I can't find the copyright assignment or remember where it came from or who drew it, because it was published before 1989 without the copyright notice, if I don't own it outright it is in the public domain and I am free to use it in my book!

What Is "Fair Use?"

"Fair use" is the legal defense to a claim against you for copyright infringement that says, hey, what I did was fair! Fair use allows you to use portions of protected works for the purpose of criticism, comment, news reporting, teaching scholarship, or research. In general, when your purpose is to comment on, not plagiarize, you are OK. You pretty much know which is which when you are creating a work.

Is Music Sampling Fair Use?

One area that has resulted in a rude education in copyright law for some is "sampling." Musicians have been taking distinctive pieces of other musicians' work and using the sample pieces in their work. Some of the samples are very short, only a few short, distinctive bars. That has to be OK, right? Wrong! So-called sampling in the creation of musical works is a big issue with artists whose work has been sampled without their permission. The courts have said that they have a right to say to other musicians, either write your own song or get permission to use mine, even a little part of mine! My advice: Don't do it without written permission!

Free Steps to Protect Your Songs, Software, and Such

When do you get a copyright? Again, a copyright exists under federal law once a work is fixed in some tangible form. That's it! All you have to do to protect your great idea by copyright is print it out, record it, or sculpt it! So long as it is an original work, you don't have to file any papers or pay any lawyers; it is protected instantly under the copyright law.

As I mentioned in Chapter 2, it used to be that if you did not know you had to, or you forgot to, put your copyright notice on the work and it was published, you lost your copyright forever! Ouch! This punitive law was changed, though, so that now you do not have to put your copyright notice on it. However, to take full advantage of the copyright law, I always advise my clients to place a copyright notice on each copy of the work. Proper notice, again, consists of three elements: (1) the symbol ©, the word *copyright,* or an abbreviation thereof; (2) the year of first publication; and (3) the name of the owner of the copyright. While you don't have to do this, it seems to me, again, that it is a whole lot easier to prove that your great idea for a painting is yours if it has your name on it! And please ignore legal advice from your friends, neighbors, advertising firm, etc. like "Ooooh don't put the copyright notice on it. It messes up the ambience!" The notice does not have to be the biggest thing on the page; it just has to be legible. For advertising proposals or other sensitive presentations, I advise putting the notice on every page!

Maximum Protection for Original Great Ideas

The defendant's lawyers arrived at the courthouse in a big, black, shiny limousine. My client and I observed this from the cramped confines of my Honda Accord. Three or four lawyers accompanied the defendant to the court room and set up shop. My client and I followed. My client was the plaintiff and was suing the defendant for infringing his copyrights to Tejano music recordings. At the very start of the case, we would have settled for a few hundred dollars and continuing royalties. Now it was different. Now it was serious. This was a federal case! I figured my client had a good case. The copyrights were registered, ownership was presumed, copying was exact. What could the defense be? Soon enough I heard it. The defense was simple enough. The big shiny lawyer said, "Judge, it can't be wrong what my client did because that's just the way things are done here in Corpus Christie in the Tejano music bidness." With my client fidgeting in the seat next to me, I rose and addressed the court and delivered the best courtroom argument of my litigation career. "Judge," I said, "last time I looked Corpus Christie was still part of Texas, and Texas is still part of the Union, and the law in the United States still applies here. We ask the court to award statutory damages for willful copyright infringement." And he did! Many thousands of dollars! This is a hint that registering the copyright to the original expression of your great idea is a very good thing most of the time!

A copyright may be registered with the federal government by filling out a simple form, paying a nominal fee, and submitting a deposit of the work. (See Appendix C for an example of how to fill out a Form VA.) Registration, again, is required in order to bring a suit to stop infringement. Also, prompt registration may entitle the copyright owner to several advantages in the event that the copyrights are infringed. Copyrights, again, currently last for the lifetime of the author plus 70 years, or 95 years from publication, or 125 from creation, whichever is less, if the work is made for hire for a business entity. (The length of a copyright demonstrates the "Golden Rule" at work in the United States. That is, He with the Gold Rules! It used to be that copyrights didn't last near as long, but Disney saw that Minnie and Donald and Goofy and company were about to become public domain property, and the life of a copyright was greatly extended! What a country!)

The advantages of registration are significant. My advice is to register your important works of art and authorship as a matter of course. Here's why. Let's say you do a drawing of your favorite place: the Newport, Rhode Island, bridge at sunset. The instant you create it in tangible form, it is protected to a minimum degree in that if you prove you created it, you can stop other people from copying it. Here is where putting your copyright notice on your original work is helpful. It should be easier to prove it is yours with your name on it, don't you think? The problem comes when you try to enforce a copyright of an unregistered work. The biggest hurdle, after you have proved you were the original artist and/or owner, is proving damages. You must prove your actual damages, and that is tough. If the infringer lost money, you can bet the court will hear about it. Damages are also hard to show if you have been selling the socks off your painting and making more money than ever. As a result, I advise taking advantage of a simpler, easier, copyright owner–friendlier option: registration!

If you apply for registration of your work within three months of publication, you qualify for "statutory damages" under copyright law. In this case, you get to tell the judge, "Judge, I don't care how much money he lost. I am asking for my statutory damages, which include court costs, attorney's fees, and statutory damages of up to $150,000 per willful infringement." Now that's what I call great leverage and a very good investment.

The thing to remember when you are considering maximizing the protection of your great idea with copyrights is that you probably won't ever get that pot of gold at the end of the infringement rainbow, but you usually won't need it because you will end the infringement so quickly. "Dear Sir: Here is a copy of my copyright registration. Please stop or die!" That's it!

The Mysterious, Little-Known "Mandatory Deposit" Requirement

Here is another reason you should register your significant works: the mandatory deposit requirement. The United States copyright office has a requirement that says that artists and authors *must* make a deposit of the work within three months of publication whether you file for registration of the copyright or not! If they see your published work and determine that you have not filed the required deposit, they can send you a letter warning you to file in three months or pay a $250 fine. If you ignore that, you will get another letter and the fine gocs up to $2,500! The good news is that filing for a copyright registration satisfies the mandatory deposit requirement, and you kill two birds with one stone!

Time and Cost

The United States Copyright Office currently charges $30 to register a copyright for your expression of your great idea. (When I started practice in 1980 it was $20. It probably costs less in real dollars today to register a copyright than it did in 1980!) The fee, a proper deposit (usually two identical specimens of the work as published), and a completed application (a simple two-sided form) are all that is required. Once you file the registration, the copyright office will examine it in due course and, usually in six months or so, you will receive the form you submitted with the registration number added to the upper right-hand corner. The date of registration is the date of submission of a complete application. It really is, usually, that simple a process.

Published versus Unpublished Works

You can file a copyright application for either an unpublished work or a work that has been published. Filing for an unpublished work is useful when you want to show someone your original work in the hope they might select it for their ad campaign, for example. A lot of effort goes into these "proposals," and while the proposal idea is not protectable, your expression of that idea is. Then, when they turn you down and turn around and use your work, you can meet them head on with a U.S. copyright registration!

Once again, all the forms and information are available at the Copyright Office Web site, *www.copyright.gov*. There are different forms for different works. For example, form TX is used for "textual" materials, such as books, and form VA is used for works of "visual arts," such as paintings. (See Appendix C for an example of how to fill out a form VA.)

One strategy for the nervous among you is to have your intellectual property attorney help you with the first copyright application. You or your secretary can then follow that successful example without further need of the attorney. Whoever does it; there can be no excuse now for not doing it! Ask yourself, is this software program worth $30? If it is, file!

5

Now Build Your Idea into Something Valuable

The whole point of this book is to explain what type of intellectual property your great idea represents and what steps you can take to protect your great idea for free! However, taking the steps I have discussed above does more than simply protect your idea; it gives you more options to work with to try to make money from your great idea! How cool is that! Let me explain.

Land a World Champion Fish, for Free!

My wife, Norma, loves to fish! My publisher, Jim Hoskins, has written a book about how to fish! I just drink beer and watch! (So far as I can tell, that is the best part about fishing.) Anyway, once you have protected your great idea for free, one option you now have is to go fishing for someone to make you an offer you can't refuse for your great idea.

The Bait

Now even if you don't fish, and even though I am not much of a fisherman, you and I both know that you just don't paddle out into the lake, the sound, or the ocean and throw your bait in the water. Fish are rude; they won't even say, "Thank you!" The same is true for trying to sell your great idea without spending a lot of money on it. If you have followed my suggestions so far, here's what you do. You draft an e-mail that says, "Dear Big Company. My name is Jim and I own the worldwide intellectual property rights to a great idea for a transportation device. (*Note:* You *do* own the worldwide intellectual property rights if you have staked a claim to your great idea as we have discussed. And even if you find out later some other guy beat you to it, it is perfectly legal to say this until you know differently!) You are Big Company, and you are in the transportation business. Last year you made $50 billion selling your stuff, but that is down 50 percent from the year before, and things aren't looking good for the new models. No offense! Anyway, my great idea for a transportation device would fit right in with your product line and add considerably to your bottom line!" Think of this part as the bait. You tell them a little about you and a little about them, and you don't need a lawyer to help you say nothing about your great idea. What you *don't* do is say, "Hey, here is a copy of my plans for an anti-gravity device; what do you think?" That is just throwing your bait in the water!

The Hook

The second part of the e-mail is the hook. It says, "If you are interested and want to hear all about my great idea and see my prototype, please send me a copy of your Non-disclosure Agreement." At this point, some of you are saying, "No way. I am sending *my own* agreement." My advice, however, is to ask the Big Company for theirs, because they have one. You could spend money on an attorney to create the perfect Non-disclosure Agreement for you, but it is a waste of money. The Big Company is just going to say, "Forget your NDA. We have spent thousands of dollars on ours, and if you want to talk with us, you'll use ours!" (This is called "the battle of the forms" in legal circles, and is a lot of fun for lawyers but not for the person paying for it!) I advise that you ask them for theirs, which shows them you know how the game is played and flatters them and all that. Just remember this: *Do not sign the big company NDA until your lawyer adds "shall not" in the appropriate places.*

You can send a zillion e-mails this afternoon to companies that might be interested in your great idea, all at no cost to you! Let's hear it for the Internet! Plus, you can keep using old bait or add new bait and go fishing again any time you like. "Hey, I didn't hear from you last month, and I have spent 10,000 hours searching the Patent Office records, and my invention sure looks patentable to me!" "Hey, I didn't hear from you, and now Shaffer has done a professional patent search, and it looks patentable to him!" "Hey, I didn't hear from you, and now I am patent pending." "Hey, my patent issued!" "HEY!" You get the idea.

The Bad News About Fishing

The bad news is that it is not likely to work! Think of it this way: How many championship, record-book fish have you ever caught? None. My wife loves fishing, and she's never caught a record fish. My publisher wrote a book about fishing, and he's not in any record books. And neither are you! The point is, just as with fishing, you are very unlikely to land the Big Company. They are, as we have discussed, invested in yesterday and they have *no interest* in the little guy. My reaction: So what? Forget the Big Company. What kinds of fish have you, my wife, my publisher, and even I caught? Little fish! Why? They are hungry! So go after the little companies too. You are much more likely to get a positive response from a little company looking to become the next Big Company.

What If You Get a Bite?

Let's say you get a bite. Some mid-sized company sends you their NDA, and your lawyer says it's OK. Now what happens? Heck if I know! But one thing I do know is that there are no "standard" anythings in any business. When a company says, "This is our standard deal," you say, "That's nice, but I want this, that, or the other thing!" Many of my clients have asked me what the standard interest rates are or the standard license fees or the standard length of a contract. There aren't any! When the Big Company reps present their "standard deal," they are telling you they think they have all the leverage because you came to them and they have all the money. So? What you must do is figure out what you want from the deal beforehand and work toward that end no matter what they say the "standard deal" is.

What kinds of deals are there? What might happen when they look at your great idea after everyone has signed the NDA? One of three basic things can happen. They can say, "Not interested. Go away." They could say, "We'll pay you $50 million for the great idea and then you go away." Or they could say, "We are not sure if it is a good idea or a great idea; let's work together to see what it might become." The first and last choices are much more likely than the second one, but hey, someone has to win the Lotto!

Bottom line: If you don't even get a nibble, this option does not place your great idea at risk, and you just might land a world champion fish for free!

Watch Your Own Cones

My law school buddy, Tom Sisson, and I were studying hard one day while watching the Wide World of Sports. It was a particularly thrilling show featuring the world championship downhill skateboard races, so you can see why we pulled ourselves away from our study of the law. Anyway, the contestants were all teenage boys, and they raced side by side down a cliff, essentially, weaving in and out between a line of orange cones on the road. Occasionally, someone would hit a cone and it would go flying. Finally, someone won, and they interviewed the winner about this and that until they asked this question: "How come those cones that the other guy hit didn't distract you?" The answer rings in my mind today just as it did then. This scruffy young kid said, "Hey man, you just got to watch your own cones!" "Watch your own cones!" These are truly words that people, especially people with a great idea, should live by!

Start an Entire New Business, for Free!

It may be that after minutes, months, or years of relentless "fishing," you decide that you have had enough fun not catching anything, and you still can't sleep at night because you know this idea is a winner. My thought is, instead of watching the other guy's cones, watch your own. Instead of trying to persuade some other company to market your idea, sell it yourself!

"United States Only" Protection Option

Let's say your research shows that the United States is the best market for your great idea. (I predict it is!) In that case, you tell yourself to forget about Csketbackinstan (wherever that might be) and the rest of the world. You focus instead on just the United States and keep your day job at the same time. Having decided to let the rest of the world go, you pick a great trademark for your great product idea. (See Chapter 2 for tips on how to pick a great brand.) You get a 16-year-old to set up a Web site for you. You figure out how much it would cost and how long it would take to make your product, and you open the site for business: "$29.99 plus postage, 90-day delivery." Then, when you get $35 million dollars in orders in the first month, you call the bank and get a loan and tell the manufacturer to start cranking them out as fast as possible. At that point you also take half of that money and spend it on your patent attorney! (Just kidding.) Then you take money out of cash flow and spend it on a patent application, a trademark application, a copyright application, and so forth. The point is, the money comes from cash flow and not your retirement or college savings fund!

On the other hand, let's say after 11 months of aggressive advertising, you haven't sold the prototype. It might still be useful, new, and non-obvious, but who cares? It's a certified commercial dog, and no amount of patent protection is going to make it hunt.

This brings up another benefit of the U.S. patent system that is not available in the rest of the so-called world. Remember, the harmonized world must rely on the marketing advice of their mothers to decide whether or not to spend the money on a patent application. The non-U.S. inventor can't actually test the product in the marketplace before spending the money on a patent application, because if they put it on the market first, it's not new anymore! How bad is that? In the United States, however, you can do this, and so long as you file the application for your great idea before a year is up, it is still new under the U.S. system!

This strategy makes perfect sense for the little guy who still has a day job! You don't even have to spend money on a trademark application for the great mark you picked because trademark rights attach with first use, and you can even wait up to three months to spend money on a copyright application! If the product cash flows, you are ready to perfect your rights to your great idea and maximize the protections available under the law. If it is a dog, forget about it!

"United States and Possibly the World" Option

I apologize to all those who believe I spend too much time worrying about the costs of protecting your great idea. I don't suppose too many of you reading this fall into that category, but if you do, sorry! Here's an option that falls between free and maximum. Let's say you have a small business and your business is generating cash flow already. Further, let's say you have determined that Canada is 65 percent of the market. Assuming these things, the best strategy is to keep the idea confidential and file a U.S. patent application, and then introduce the product into the market. If the product takes off, you can still file in Canada! This is because you followed the rest of the world's rule that you must keep your great idea confidential and file a patent application first, and *then* bring the product to market. Because you followed their rule, by international treaty they give you a year from the U.S. application date within which to file an application in their country.

This is an option chosen by most companies for ideas that their research shows should do well in the U.S. as well as in other countries. They have the cash flow to support the cost of the patent application, and by following the rest of the world's rules they keep their options open to file in the rest of the world. It could be that three months after you have introduced your great idea into the U.S. market the rest of the world asks, "Do you have the rights to Canada?" "Yes," you say. "Will $10 million be enough to buy the rights to Canada?" "Let me think about it," you say, adding, "Anybody interested in Japan?" How about that for a happy fantasy!

World Domination Option

This option is for the "money is no object" group or the "surefire winner" great idea. The most conservative option for protecting your great idea is to spend the money on a patent application in the United States and the relevant foreign countries (read "countries in which you know the product will sell") after you have kept your idea confidential. This gets you started in the lengthy process right away, which means you will get a patent (if you do) sooner, not later!

Prior to introducing your product into the market, you also file your trademark application based on a "bona fide intent to use" the mark in commerce in the United States and the desired relevant foreign markets. You file your copyright application right away on your $60,000 ad, and it is respected in every country in the world and you have signed NDAs from everyone you have discussed the idea with. Your employees have all signed trade secret agreements, and no one knows anything about the idea unless they have a need to know! At that point, you launch your patent-pending product, and it is as protected as it can be during the period before you know whether the patent will issue.

This option does make sense for great ideas that can't wait, because the truth is that the sooner you file the applications—patent, trademark, and copyright—the sooner they are likely to issue. You also have the entire world available for patent protection, plus you are ahead of the game with regard to trademarks and copyrights. While the other strategies have a wait-and-see element, this one does not. It also appeals to the covert, behind-the-scenes types who like to get all the heavy lifting done before letting anyone else know they are up to something!

Licenses

Once your great idea is protected, you have the ability to license it to the highest bidder. The idea behind a license is that you let the other guy do all the work and they pay you! Sounds good to me! A license is a contractual agreement to allow someone to do something that would be illegal for them to do without the license. How's that for genuine legalese? The point is, once you have protected your great idea, without your permission no one can make, sell, or use your great idea, or copy it, or use the same or a similar brand for it.

There Is No "Standard" License

One of the questions I hear all the time is: "What is the standard license for this type of idea?" Again, the truth is that there is *no* standard license for anything. Anytime someone tells you, "This is our standard license," what they are really telling you is "We have more leverage than you do!" If all you have is a raw idea and you have taken no steps to protect it, you have almost no leverage and you are pretty much at the mercy of whomever you are dealing with. If, however, you have taken at least the minimum free steps to protect your great idea, you can say, "That is very interesting and a good place to start, but I own the worldwide intellectual property rights to this great idea, and I was thinking more along the lines of..."

Think "Just Playing Poker!"

Once you have protected your idea, getting the best license for it is the result of "just playing poker!" (See Figure 5.1.) By that I mean you have staked a claim to your idea, and that is what you are holding in your "hand." The company/ person you are dealing with holds something you want in their hand, usually money or manufacturing capability. You want them to "bet" first, and that is what their "standard" license is to be viewed as—just their first bet. You can expect it to be low! I tell my clients that their response to any offer, no matter

Figure 5.1. Getting the best license for your idea is the result of "just playing poker."

what it is, should be "Oh, well, I will consider $35 million, of course, but I was expecting a much higher starting point!" Always act disappointed! Never start dancing and singing in front of them! Keep your poker face on!

What Should You Ask for in a License?

The question, then, is what should you ask for? Every great idea is different, and every licensing situation is driven by the particular facts and circumstances surrounding it. Nonetheless, there are some things that you should consider asking for in every licensing situation.

What Do You Want?

First, you should write down what you want! You would be surprised how many of my clients have never stopped to consider what they really want out of the agreement. I know for sure that you will not get what you want from a license if you don't know what you want to ask for. So start by making a list of things you want. Then prioritize them, realizing that you will not get everything you ask for. Some things are "deal breakers," which you must have or there is no deal, and others are things you ask for but you can really do without. You might want to be head of sales. Well, you won't get it if you don't ask for it, but it is usually not something you can hold out for and still get a license. On the other hand, you might want product development oversight, and that could be something to hold out for!

Three Types of Payments to Ask For

There are three types of payments that you should ask for in a license. The first is a "lump-sum" payment. The lump-sum payment comes at the start of the agreement; right after it is signed, hopefully. It represents the amount of leverage the person with the great idea has in the deal. The more leverage, the higher the payment. The payment can be thought of as representing a number of things: recovery of development costs, sweat equity, lost economic opportunity, and so forth. What it really is, again, is a measure of the amount of leverage you have in the deal.

The next thing to ask for is a "minimum" royalty. A minimum royalty is a fee that the licensee (the person getting the license from you) pays the licensor (you, the person giving the license) the first of every month, for example, whether or not the licensee has sold any product or not! How great is that! Again, the amount of the minimum royalty, and even its very existence, is a measure of your leverage in the deal. It is a very important part of a license for the person with the great idea because even if the company doesn't sell a thing, they must still send you a check. As a result, it is insurance against a company signing the license and doing nothing with your great idea. Every minimum royalty check they write is motivation for them to get out there and make your great idea the best-selling thing they have ever marketed!

The third thing to ask for is an "earned" royalty. An earned royalty is what most folks think of when they think of payments they will receive from a license. The way it works is, the company pays you a minimum royalty of $2,000 on the first of the month. Then, on the fifteenth of each month, they calculate what they sold and what percentage they owe you. If they sold less than $2,000 worth of royalties, you don't get an earned royalty check and they get heartburn. If they sold $20,000 worth of royalties, you get another check for $18,000. Sweet!

Forget Good; What If Things Go Bad?

Many other things can and do go into a typical license agreement. For example, what happens if things don't go as planned? It is common at the beginning of a deal for everyone to focus on the happy future. Still, things don't always go as expected, and it is a good idea to pay attention to how you can back out of the deal if you want to! Very often, a license will include performance milestones and deadlines, for example, that the licensee must meet in order to keep the license.

Pigs Get Fed and Hogs Get Slaughtered

The truth is, with a new great idea, it is often very difficult to anticipate the future. As the owner of the great idea, you are the most optimistic about how it will do. You had better be optimistic, because if you are not, no one else will be, that is for sure! Still, you cannot guarantee that it will sell like hotcakes. This is the point you will hear most often from the licensee. They will be very skeptical. So now what do you do? You think it will go great but you can't guarantee it, and they think it might not go great but it might! What you do not want is a long-term license at an unfairly low royalty rate, and they don't want a long-term license at an unfairly high royalty rate. The way out of this dilemma is to keep the initial term of the license as short as possible. Rather than holding out for a high royalty and losing the deal altogether, it is a much better strategy to accept a lower royalty rate for a short period of time. That way the company is not at such a high risk of paying for a commercial bomb and they are more likely to do the deal. If it turns out the product is as great as you imagined and you got less than you should have, well, it won't last long! At the end of the first term, you will have all the leverage you need to get the deal you want and deserve for your great idea! I like this approach to a license—keeping the initial term short—because it is more likely to result in at least getting a deal. And in my opinion, it is better to get some deal at lower-than-desired rates for a short term than no deal at all! Particularly if you still have your day job! As they still say in Texas, remember, pigs get fed and hogs get slaughtered.

What Is the Difference Between a License and an Assignment?

I notice that a lot of my clients are confused by the terms "license" and "assignment." The easy way to approach it is to think of your great idea as your house. If you rent your house out, you get paid by others to use it, but you still own it. If they mess it up or don't pay, you get your house back. This is what a license is, a rental agreement. On the other hand, if you sell your house, you get paid for it and then you no longer have any control over it. The new owners can burn it down or build it up, and you can't say a word. This is what an assignment is, a sales agreement. Which one is best for you and your great idea depends on you and your circumstances. My advice is, don't sign anything until your wife/husband and lawyer look it over!

"Cease to Exist" Letters: Think "Oh Happy Day!"

I could tell my client was mad. Because the veins on his neck were standing out and his face was beet red and he was screaming, I knew he was really mad. He had come into my office telling me that he wanted me to send a "cease to exist" letter to a competitor for copying his ad. This much I knew. I had helped protect the ad by copyright, and his competitor had pretty much copied it exactly. What I couldn't understand is what he wanted me to do. Although I had lived in Texas for at least 15 years, I thought maybe it was some local-custom thing that irate cowboys had been doing for years. "Cease to exist?" I said. "What is that?" He said, "You know, lawyers send them to folks who mess with their client's stuff and tell them to stop!" "Oh, I get it," I said. "You want me to send them a 'cease and desist' letter." He agreed that that was what he wanted, and because he had protected his idea by copyright, I was able to send a very strong letter suggesting that the copying must stop immediately, among other things.

Ever since then, I have always thought of these as "cease to exist" letters. If you have taken at least some baby steps to protect your great idea, you will have the leverage you need to send a "cease to exist" letter to your number one competitor who has messed with your great idea illegally! What you want most in a conflict situation is clear evidence that you have the leverage necessary to end the conflict in your favor. You want the other guy to stop and you don't want to have to go to court to make them stop. Of course, the more leverage you have, the more strongly worded your letter can be. Armed with registered trademarks, copyrights, patents, and trade secret agreements, it can truly add up to a demand that your competitor "cease to exist!"

6

What If I Am an Employee with a Great Idea?

It may seem that this book is only for businesses or independent individuals, and that anyone who happens to work for someone else (i.e., most of us) is simply out of luck when it comes to having a great idea. Not true! This chapter is specifically for employees. You will discover what you can and should do to set up a perfect claim to your great idea, no matter whom you work for.

Do Employees and Great Ideas Go Together?

Jet fuel in a water fountain; strawberry ice cream and rum; deaf, blind cats and cars; Great Danes and ski rope; Dalmatians and calm: This is a short list of things that I know for a fact from my personal experience *do not go together*! On the other hand, employees and great ideas can go together very nicely. Just be careful what you sign!

Have You Signed a Contract?

People who work for others may think that the combination of their status as an employee and their ownership of a great idea don't go together either. Many people with great ideas work for other people. These people often end up in my office asking me what rights they have to their great idea. I tell them, in classic lawyerese, as you have learned, that it depends! Mostly it depends on whether or not they signed an employment contract. Remember, if you are offered an employment contract to sign before you start work somewhere, rule number one is: Don't sign anything until you have read it twice and know what it means. Most employment contracts these days include agreements as to the ownership of "intellectual property" developed during employment. Typically, these agreements are to the effect that if you think of a great idea after signing the contract, related to your job or not, the company owns it. My advice is, *do not* sign such a contract if you can avoid it. If you can't avoid it altogether, maybe you can modify it to cover only "job-related" ideas or ideas developed on company time with company resources. Otherwise, when you invent the cure to cancer on your day off from parking cars, the company has a legal claim to that invention! You might be able to convince a court that the contract was unfair or overreaching, but courtrooms are very expensive places to be. The best thing to do is to eliminate the chance of that happening right at the start before signing the contract.

Again, most employment contracts do cover who owns what in the event that the employee develops a great idea. Many contracts make perfectly good sense. "We hired you to invent a cure to cancer, and you did. We own it." That makes sense. Many contracts also provide reasonable loopholes. Many companies let their employees keep the ideas they come up with if they are not related to the company's business. "Your great idea relates to an anti-gravity device and has nothing to do with the company's search for the cure to cancer. You own it." That makes sense too!

What If You Have a Great Idea Before You Sign a Contract?

Often, an employee joins a company at a time when the employee already has a great idea. In that case, the employee should make an addendum to the contract listing all of the employee's previous ideas that are to be excluded from the scope of the contract. Then, while you agree that anything you come up with in the future is theirs, the great ideas you had before joining them are clearly yours. In other cases, companies have intellectual property review boards that evaluate ideas from their employees. In such a case, even ideas related to the company business may be released to the employee if the review board says the company is not interested in them.

Many companies and universities are adopting progressive compensation packages for their employees with great ideas. This makes sense too, does it not? The employee is encouraged to innovate, and the company gets enthusiastic innovators! Some companies and universities pay for each invention disclosure, for each patent application, and for each issued patent. Some also pay a percentage of income from the idea.

The bottom line for employees is to carefully read the employment contract *before* signing it! Once you sign it, it is enforceable against you, and you may have lost your great idea forever!

What If You Don't Have an Employment Contract?

It is true that many companies don't have employment contracts. Does that mean you own every great idea you come up with while working for them? Not necessarily! Companies get "shop rights" to ideas you come up with on their time and with their resources, even without a contract. A shop right is a right the law imposes on the inventor allowing the company that essentially paid for the idea to use it. The company cannot apply for a patent or make or sell the idea, but they can use it in their "shop." Without a contract, though, every other great idea you come up with on your own time with your own resources is yours. Let's say you are employed by a cancer cure company to park cars, and you signed no contract. Then, at home in your kitchen sink, you develop the cure to cancer. You own it! Your great idea is yours, and your car parking days are over!

7

Meet Jim H (a Hypothetical Guy with a Great Idea and No Money)

When it comes to understanding the meaning of a contract, my advice is to give an example. Following my own advice, in this chapter I illustrate what we have discussed so far with an example of what a person with a great idea, and no extra funds to finance it, can do to protect and profit from his great idea, step by step.

Optimism Meets FUD

I am an optimistic person. I actually believe Navy will beat Notre Dame in football again! But this optimism pales to insignificance compared with the optimism characteristic of people who have a great idea! Unfortunately, all this happy optimism is usually overwhelmed by FUD. As my good friend Dr. Ray Smilor explained to me, FUD stands for *Fear*, *Uncertainty*, and *Doubt*. Everybody has some amount of FUD, but people with a great idea seem to have more than their fair share. One of the major reasons for the existence of this book, in fact, is to eliminate FUD for folks who have a great idea! So here is an example of how a hypothetical person with a great idea and no money to burn can proceed to try to make something of his idea while keeping FUD to a minimum.

First the Discovery—Then the Paranoia!

Mr. Jim H (for Hypothetical) wakes up from a deep sleep in a cold sweat. He's finally figured it out! After all those days, weeks, years, anti-gravity is his! He has figured out the secret to gravity, and the result is his great idea for an anti-gravity device! Oh joy! Jim's joy, however, is met immediately by massive FUD! With no budget and no willingness to quit his day job just yet, what can he do to protect this great idea? Deeply paranoid and trusting no one, Jim is one sad idea man. Then he recalls a little book he read once stating that there are free things he can do to start to protect his great idea. He begins to breathe again and takes the first free steps to protect his great idea.

Do the Free Stuff First—Then Take a Deep Breath and Relax

First Jim gets three folders. In the first folder he puts a completed invention disclosure form that explains what problem he has solved, what others have done to solve the problem as far as he is aware, and what he has done to solve the problem, along with sketches or drawings of the invention. Most important, Jim gets the disclosure witnessed by two people (preferably not his mom and wife), and he keeps the disclosure confidential!

Jim is naturally paranoid, and he knows instinctively that it is important to keep his idea confidential and not go blabbing it around. But he also needs to talk to some people about developing his great idea. So when he needs help for his great idea or wants to talk with someone about it, he always has the person sign a Non-disclosure Agreement first. Jim places the signed NDAs in the second folder.

Next, instead of watching sports all weekend, like he usually does, Jim spends most of his free time aggressively investigating the commercial viability of his anti-gravity invention on the Internet. Who is in the business or related businesses? What is being sold, and for how much? Where are these pathetic old-technology things being sold? How much will it cost to make his anti-gravity device? Who can make it? Any and all information that is relevant to his great idea goes in folder number three. Jim knows that "knowledge is power" and that you never know when what you know is going to be useful!

Jim's great idea for an anti-gravity invention will be safe once he has created a signed, dated, witnessed invention disclosure form. He knows that is all he has to do to create tangible evidence that he had the great idea at least as early as the date of the invention disclosure. Because there is no race to the Patent

Office in the United States, and because we have a "first to invent" system, Jim will have greatly reduced his FUD associated with his great idea. Making sure to keep his great idea confidential is another FUD reducer, and showing or describing his great idea to people only *after* they have agreed in writing to keep it confidential is yet another FUD reducer. On top of that, by taking these free steps Jim keeps his options open for worldwide protection! Big-time FUD reducer! Finally, knowing the potential cost-benefit of his idea by knowing the market in detail pretty much eliminates the remainder of Jim's FUD.

At this point, Jim's FUD is minimal and his optimism is high, but Jim still has no budget. Now what?

Go Fishing for Free

Because he has no money and he is not ready to spend his five kids' college funds on his great idea just yet, Jim takes a stab at making money from his great idea without spending a dime. He takes out folder number three and goes fishing! He drafts an e-mail in two parts. The first part is the bait. He tells a little about himself and a little about the addressee: "Hi. I am a very smart ex-IBM guy with an inquisitive mind. In my spare time, when I wasn't surfing with dolphins in beautiful Hilton Head, South Carolina, I developed an anti-gravity device. You are the world's third largest airline, and not doing so well lately according to your public filings. I believe my product could help you out!" What Jim *does not* say is "And here is a copy of the plans!" Jim knows that would just be feeding his idea to the fish!

The second part is the hook, and it says, "If you are interested and want to fly me and my patent attorney to Hawaii for two weeks [Jim knows that he must never forget his helpful and patient patent attorney, even if he hasn't hired one yet!] to tell you all about my idea, please send me a copy of your Non-disclosure Agreement." He knows that the company he is addressing most likely has an NDA. They would ignore one that he might send. and Jim would have wasted his money spent preparing his own NDA. He knows the most important thing in this exercise is that he must *not* sign their NDA, however, until he and his lawyer have looked it over. Jim knows that this e-mail is a long shot, but he rightly figures that someone has to catch the championship fish and, besides, it's free! Jim knows that it doesn't hurt to try this approach and that he can fish without FUD for as long as he likes. He can add new "bait" if he wishes or fish with the same bait the whole time. At some point, if Jim tires of fishing, he can quit! He may have had no luck making any money from his raw idea, but he has not done any harm to himself or risked his great idea in any way. Completely FUD-free—just the way Jim likes it!

A Good Hard Look in the Mirror

Let's say that Jim got no nibbles at all from his e-mail bait. Still, he is not discouraged. In fact, he has already improved the original anti-gravity device so that it now doubles as a hair dryer for his wavy surfer hair. His problem now is that he is losing sleep at night from constantly thinking about his idea. He knows it will go big in the market! Unfortunately, though, he has no dough and he is not ready to quit his cushy job working from home just yet. What to do? He takes a good hard look in the mirror. (A very scary thing for Jim and most people!) He evaluates his situation, and he remembers reading somewhere that he can try to market the idea himself. He knows he doesn't even need a prototype or a warehouse full of anti-gravity hair dryers (AGHDs). From his third folder, with all his research, he pulls out the costs he has determined to be associated with making the AGHD, and the time it would take the local machine shop to get one made, and he sets a selling price for it.

Then Jim does the smart thing and picks a great brand for his revolutionary device: PINK PELICAN flying hair dryers. Next, he has his high school-age son work up a Web site, creates an original ad using his lovely wife to demo the product, and lets 'er rip, as they say in Texas. "Let PINK PELICAN brand flying hair dryers set you and your hair free for only $99.99 down and $9.99 a month for nine months. Allow 99 days for delivery!" When he gets $35 million in orders in the first month, he goes to the bank and gets an advance. Then he calls the shop and tells them to start making them as fast as they can. Then he calls his patent attorney and says, "Bingo!" Jim knows he gave up the right to get patents in foreign countries for this idea because he didn't file a patent application before he made his idea public. Still, he knows there are more great ideas where that one came from, and having the best market in the world for his first great idea is not all that bad.

Suppose, however, after 11 months of aggressive advertising he still hasn't sold one PINK PELICAN flying hair dryer. Jim knows that it still may be patentable technically, but who cares? He sure doesn't, and now he knows no one else does either. The good news, though, is that he found this out without having spent a dime up front on a patent application, a trademark application, or a copyright application while having protected his great idea in several different ways for free the whole time. And all as FUD-less as you can get for free!

At Some Point, Early or Late, It's All About Cash Flow

It goes without saying in a book about how to protect your great idea for free, that in the end, it's all about cash flow. What I mean is, great ideas are great and all that, but you have a life, and no great idea is worth going bankrupt over. Better to let some other person or company go bankrupt over your great idea than you, that's my thought! So assuming you are a real person, with a real job and real bills to pay and a real life to lead, the time to stop messing with an idea, no matter how great it may seem to you, is when it does not translate to cash flow. It may be great and all, but if you have to start paying more than a little to keep it alive, let it die!

On the other hand, when it starts to bring in money, then it is time to gaze into the crystal ball and see what kind of future it may have. Once you are confident that it is a winner and that the cash flow is sure to continue, start putting money aside for maximizing protection for the idea. Take all your information to your intellectual property lawyer and get the ball rolling toward getting all the protection you can under the law. Look at the time that has elapsed from the introduction of the product to the marketplace, and be sure to file a patent application, if warranted, before a year has gone by. File an application for registration of your great brand and a copyright application for your great ad. Make sure all your new employees sign an employment agreement that requires them to keep your great trade secrets secret. Then sit back and smell the deposit slips!

8

Questions I Hear and You Should Ask

People I meet in social settings never seem bashful about asking me any type of legal question once they find out I am a lawyer. Strangely, when clients come into my office to meet with me, they often fail to ask me even the most basic questions. This chapter lists some of the questions people do ask and some they don't ask but should!

Top 10 Questions Clients Ask

Sometimes you can't guess what people are thinking or what they are going to say. For example, my wife, Norma, was checking out of the grocery store one day after leaving her job as a speech pathologist. The checker eyed her badge and said, "You're a speech pathologist?" and Norma said, "Why, yes, I am," and the checker said, "Wow! So you can speak to the dead?" This happened in the great state of Texas and can probably be put down to too much time in the sun. Anyway, while I often can't guess what people are thinking, lots of times I can tell with certainty what a new client is going to ask. Over the years I have come up with a top 10 list of questions I am sure to be asked at one time or another by a client. Here they are, in reverse order:

    10. (tie) How 'bout them Middies?! And do you think this is the year Navy finally beats Notre Dame?

Actually, no one has ever been so bold as to ask me this. But I know they are thinking it!

9. Since my employees have signed a non-compete agreement, I don't need them to sign a trade secret agreement, do I?

Oh yes you do and should. See Chapter 2 for a full explanation.

8. Since I paid for the ad, I own the copyright, don't I?

Maybe not! See Chapters 2 and 4.

7. Well, obviously I can use my own name as a brand, can't I?

Not necessarily! See Chapter 2.

6. My brand describes my product. That's good, right?

Extra-big No! See Chapter 2 again.

5. Since I have already incorporated, I really don't need to register my brand, do I?

Yes you do, if you can! Refer to Chapter 2.

4. Is the invention development company I saw on TV legitimate?

Not likely! See Chapter 3.

3. What do you think of my invention?

This is similar to the next question on the list. I just tell my clients what I think, with the caveat that I have done this long enough to know I cannot accurately predict the future. If I could, I would be living in Las Vegas!

2. Is my idea patentable?

When my clients ask me this, they really are asking me to predict if the patent examiner would grant them a patent for the idea. I tell them what I think, of course, but I also tell them it really is not my opinion that counts; it is the patent examiner they must convince! Then I say if it meets the three tests for patentability, it is for sure patentable!

1. What does it cost?

   By far the most often asked question! I tell them, it depends! First, I must come to understand their great idea, and then I will give them an estimate.

Top Five Questions Clients Should Ask!

Have you ever heard the expression "Don't check your brain at the door?" Well, it is a perfect description of what not to do when you meet a lawyer! Don't check your brain at the door! While it is true that most people never have the need to meet with a lawyer and, therefore, when you meet one for the first time it can be a nervous situation, lawyers are just people! They can't read your mind any more than you can read theirs. So ask lots of questions! Make a list of questions to ask before you get to the meeting. Ask whatever you want! And here are my suggestions for questions that should be on every list:

1. What Is Your Background and Experience?

Many folks think every lawyer does every type of legal thing. Not true. Like doctors, lawyers specialize. Some lawyers deal only with bankruptcies. Some deal only with deaths. In fact, I like what I do very much because from my perspective, it seems that most lawyers are fighting over dead things—dead businesses, dead contracts, dead people! And I don't care how good of a lawyer they may be, when all is said and done the person is still dead! I think that is what leaves a bitter taste in people's mouths after most of their encounters with lawyers, through no fault of the lawyer. "Gee, I paid him all that money and, you know, Dad's still dead!" I think of what I do, however, as working in the baby wing of the hospital. No one is ever mad at a brand new little baby idea, and I help protect it! It may not grow up into anything, but at least I can give it the chance to! Anyway, another thing to know is that even specialists special-ize. Not every patent attorney can or should handle every kind of great idea for an invention, for example. If the great idea is a chemical something, you want a lawyer with a chemical background. If the idea is a mechanical invention or a new life-form or a new ad campaign, whatever it is, there are lawyers that are best suited for the job. So ask, what is your background?

Next ask, what is your experience? Every brain surgeon must have his or her first patient; I just don't want it to be me! I am not saying that intellectual property law is brain surgery, but experience is a very practical teaching tool, and usually the more experience your lawyer has, the better! I would be wary of letting the intellectual property lawyer fresh out of school handle my cancer cure idea, for example. He or she might be perfect for a simple dog bowl patent but not for a revolutionary technology. On the other hand, watch out for the seasoned lawyer with one foot in retirement! In short, you want someone who's been "in the game" long enough to know the rules but not someone who has played so long as to be played out!

2. How Do You Bill, and for What?

You might be surprised to know that many people don't even ask what they will be billed for. When dealing with a lawyer, you should have a written agreement that explains how the lawyer bills, at what rates, and for what. Many, if not most, lawyers, in addition to their hourly rate, bill for sending and receiving a fax, for long-distance calls, for copies, for postage, etc. I don't. I am not saying it is wrong to do so, but I am too old now to mess with the job of keeping track of all that! My hourly rate covers the "overhead," so my bills are simple compared with those of some other lawyers. In any event, as with any contract, *do not* sign the agreement with the lawyer until you completely understand how they bill and for what!

3. Which Lawyer in the Firm Will Actually Do the Work?

Most clients believe that the lawyer they contact and/or meet at the law firm is the same lawyer who will do the work for them. Not necessarily! Sometimes the big-name partner brings the client in and then hands the work off to the brand-new law school graduate. This is not a problem if the lawyer working on the matter is the most qualified to do so. But sometimes the young associate does the work and bills for it, and the senior lawyer reviews the work and bills for it, and the client ends up paying for two lawyers instead of one! This is still not a problem if the client knows this is going to happen in advance, and the total is within the estimate the client accepted! So ask, which lawyer is actually going to do the work?

4. Do You Give Estimates of the Fees?

Most lawyers have an hourly rate and bill in increments of an hour, say tenths. That is, their minimum bill for doing work for their clients is a tenth of their hourly rate. Every six minutes or part thereof amounts to a tenth of an hour worked! Lawyers keep track of their billable hours—or "billable owls" as John Sullivan calls them. (See Chapter 4, Figure 4.1). Even if your lawyer is working on a project without an estimate, he or she should be able to give you an idea of a range of time that will be spent on the project. My belief is that a client's biggest fear is that the lawyer will spend a lot of time on something the client had no idea was required. What the client does *not* want is a $10,000 bill for research showing up unexpectedly. I prefer to give estimates for every job I accept. It is not a flat or guaranteed fee, but it is very close to that, and that way surprises are kept to a minimum.

Some lawyers will do "contingent fee" agreements, where the lawyer pays all the expenses, or the client pays or shares in some of the expenses, and the lawyer is paid only if there is a recovery. This is the usual case with personal injury law, for example. Some intellectual property lawyers will also take a contingent interest in their client's great idea instead of fees. Other lawyers charge a flat rate for certain services.

Whatever the arrangement, you should always have at least an estimate of the fees involved, and the bill you get for the work done for you should never be a big surprise!

5. Are Any Retainers Refundable?

Just because you give a lawyer a "retainer" doesn't mean the lawyer will retain any of it to give back to you if you change your mind! You must ask whether or not the retainer is "refundable" or "non-refundable." With a refundable retainer any amount of money you give a lawyer is held in a trust account under your name for your benefit until the lawyer earns the money by doing the work you asked him or her to do. At any point before the work is completed, if you say stop, the lawyer will send the balance of the funds back to you! A non-refundable retainer, of course, does not come back to you. That is, although the lawyer obviously expected to finish the work, if you say stop in a non-refundable arrangement, the work stops but the money does not come back to you! So ask, is the money I give you refundable?

One Question for You (and the Answer Will Surprise You)

With all this talk about leverage and stopping conflicts and all that, many of my clients actually get a little excited about the prospect of a big-time knock-down, drag-out courtroom drama to enforce their new rights! That's when I say, "I bet you a nickel that you have never sued anyone in your entire life!" If I had collected that nickel every time I won the bet I would be rich! The thing is, if you watch TV you may think that everybody in America has sued everybody else at least 10 times. Not true! In fact, most people have never sued anyone. We work things out if the neighbors' dog gets in our yard, we don't sue them! As a result, most folks don't have any idea how downright miserable a lawsuit is, how much time it takes, how much money it costs, and how unpredictable the results can be even with a "good case." My hope for you, gentle reader, is that you may never have to participate in a lawsuit. Even if you win, it is still highly annoying and a big waste of time and energy.

With that said, who does file lawsuits? Companies! Why? It's not because companies are big meanies, although some are, but it is because the boundaries between intellectual properties are separated by legal tests that are often subjective analyses, as we have discussed. The boundary between trademarks, again, is: Is there a likelihood of confusion between our two products in the innocent consumer's mind? The companies may try to work it out but still end up unable to agree. How do they solve that dispute? In some cultures, they whip out swords and have at it; in other cultures, the side with the closest ties to the dictator wins; in the United States, we go to court! (It amuses me when people say, "Americans are so litigious." Well, yes, that's our system! We laid down our sixguns, and now we let a judge and jury decide the conflicts we can't resolve ourselves. It works for me!)

I assure you that if your great idea results in a commercially successful business, at one time or another a conflict with a competitor will arise that you can't resolve. At that point, as I have said, you want to have the leverage necessary to end the conflict quickly, inexpensively, and in your favor. With sufficient leverage, hopefully you won't ever have to go to court, but if you have to you will win!

9

Final Thoughts

Well, except for this last chapter and the appendices, stick a fork in you, you are done! Still, I do have some additional thoughts and comments for you to consider. This chapter serves as a brief reality check along with a few final words of encouragement for you and your great idea!

It Just Doesn't Matter!

By now I knew that my boss, Jim Koehn, was depressed. I could hear the little handheld tape recorder playing a segment from a Chevy Chase movie over and over and over. I don't remember the name of the movie, but Chevy was a camp counselor for the poor group of kids across the lake from the rich kids' camp, and they were going to have a camp competition. Chevy's "pep" talk was: "It just doesn't matter. They have all the money and they are going to get all the girls and it just doesn't matter!" So his kids started chanting, "It just doesn't matter, it just doesn't matter!" That slogan became their rallying cry, and they won the camp championship for the first time ever! Anyway, every time something bad happened to my boss he would start playing that pep talk!

The point is, sometimes even with the best possible protection, things don't go exactly as planned or predicted. I won't tell you that if you follow all the things I have discussed in this book your great idea is guaranteed to prevail in a conflict! It may, in fact, not be enough to win the day. It wasn't for one of my clients who had a surefire winner of a case! Read on!

Bubba Did Not Like It!

We had the law, facts, and good witnesses on our side in the trademark infringement case. My client owned the mark BUBBA LIKES IT for restaurant services. Some folks who previously actually had worked with my client started a restaurant called BUBBA'S. The client had evidence of actual confusion in innocent consumers' minds as to whether or not the new restaurant was my client's. My client was respectable and presentable, and not crazy! When the other side would not agree to stop using the term Bubba's, we sued, confident of victory. And we lost! It is a good example to keep in mind whenever you are thinking of suing anyone: You may lose no matter how strong your case seems to you and your lawyer! Ouch!

Having said that, though, we all know life is a risk and there are no guarantees. So assuming you are not put off by the chance of failure, what have some other people with great ideas done in the face of rejection and defeat?

You Just Might Not Be Crazy!

These people, at least, stuck with their ideas. When the world said, "No, you can't!" they said, "Oh yes I can!"

This person with a great idea was 65 years old. He had during his life failed at selling insurance, tires, and food. He couldn't make it as a fireman, a sailor, or a service station operator. He tried food again and sold out his interest for a pittance. He was left to live on his $105 Social Security check. And then what did he do? He tried his great idea one more time at the age of 65, and the result? KFC! In his final effort at making a success of his life, he went restaurant to restaurant cooking up chicken with his secret recipe, and if they liked it, they would pay him five cents a chicken. In 12 years he had more than 600 franchised outlets, and by the time he sold his last business, he was a multimillionaire!

This person was having problems with his computer class in college. The professor said he couldn't do what he said he wanted to do. So he quit school and formed Dell Computers while he was selling something like $35,000 a week in computers out of the back of his car!

Chester Carlson and Xerox. Bill Gates and Microsoft. Big names with great ideas, and generally speaking, the world ignored them or pooh-poohed their ideas! So do not take it personally if everyone tells you that you and your great idea are nuts! It happens all the time and the pundits/know-it-alls are very often wrong. Remember, they are focused on yesterday, not tomorrow!

Imagine If Anyone Had Listened to These Pundits

Trust yourself and your great idea! You have a vision that the world may be unable to see no matter how obvious it is to you! Here are some comments on great ideas for your consideration:

- *"There is no reason anyone would want a computer in their home."*—Ken Olson, president, chairman, and founder of Digital Equipment Corporation

- *"This telephone has too many shortcomings to be seriously considered as a means of communication."*—Western Union internal memo, 1876

- *"Heavier than air flying machines are impossible."*—Lord Kelvin, president, Royal Society, 1895

- *"Who wants to hear actors talk?"*—H.M. Warner, Warner Brothers, 1927

- *"Louis Pasteur's theory of germs is ridiculous fiction."*—Pierre Pachet, professor of physiology at Toulousse, 1872

- *"Drill for oil? You mean drill into the ground to try to find oil? You're crazy!"*—Drillers whom Edwin L. Drake tried to enlist in his project to drill for oil, 1859

And my personal favorite:

- *"Everything that can be invented has been invented."*—Charles H. Duell, Commissioner, U.S. Office of Patents, 1899

So when they say you are crazy, they may be right, of course, but they may not—and they just might not know as much about you and your great idea as you do! And remember the words of a man who repeated grade school because he was bad at English and then went on to become one of the greatest public speakers of all time and to lead England to victory in World War II:

"Never give up! Never, ever, give up!"—Winston Churchill

Finally, Think Dressing for Cold Weather

As we have discussed, there are multiple ways to protect great ideas. Keeping your great idea for an invention confidential allows possible worldwide protection for it as it is developed. Knowing how to pick a great brand makes it easy to protect the brand from future competitors and ensures that customers who want your product can find it easily amidst all the similar products. Knowing the difference between a work for hire and that of an independent contractor keeps your great idea yours and makes sure you own what you pay for. Simply keeping your secrets "secret" is a great start to protecting your great idea. In short, at every stage of development of your great idea, your objective should be to protect it in as many different ways as possible. Remember, the more layers of protection you have, the longer you can stay out in the cold. The same is true for your great idea.

About the Author

Nevin and Norma Shaffer have two children ages 18 and 12, live in Gulf Breeze, Florida and have two goofy cats named Tony and Chico.

Nevin is an eagle scout, one of the few people who actually bought a ticket to Woodstock and is a retired navy commander who served in Vietnam.

He has an engineering physics degree from the United States Naval Academy, has an MBA from the University of Houston, and earned his juris doctorate degree in law from St. Mary's School of Law in San Antonio, Texas. He is a licensed patent attorney in all 50 states and is licensed in Texas and Florida as well. He has been a patent lawyer for 26 years.

Nevin has a passion for helping individuals and small businesses! He believes that the same business protections provided to the large corporations of our country can and should be used to protect the individual and small business as well.

Appendix A

Doing Your Own Trademark Search

The focus of this book is how to protect your great idea for free. The good news is just that: You can take steps to protect your great idea that don't cost you anything and don't require a lawyer. The bad news is, you will have to *do* something! This is not for everyone, I know! The really busy or faint of heart will always be the lawyer's friend. But if you have time and energy, you can do a lot in the way of protecting your idea with a good brand for free! Here are examples of resources you can use to search your brand, both federal and state, and ways to use your brand properly too!

Federal Trademark Searches Are Much More Accurate than Patent Searches

The U.S. Patent and Trademark Office works diligently to update its records, always remaining no more than a few weeks or so behind, so they say! Trademark applications are not confidential, and pending trademark applications may be searched, unlike most pending patent applications. This is why trademark searches that can be done for free on the Internet are more accurate than patent searches. Don't get me wrong; nothing is perfect, and you may miss something, but the chances of finding problems with your mark right off the bat are good!

A Sample Federal Trademark Search for PINK PELICAN

Let's say Jim H (remember the guy with the flying hair dryer idea? See Chapter 7) wants to see if the mark he wants to use, PINK PELICAN, is available.

Step 1. You go to your (by now) favorite Web site, www.uspto.gov, but this time you go to the Trademark Office part and click "Trademarks." (Figure A.1)

Step 2. Next you click on the term "Search." (Figure A.2)

Step 3. Next you click on "New User Form Search (Basic)." (Figure A.3) There are other, more sophisticated ways to search that you can mess with later, but for now, my advice is to keep it simple!

Step 4. This brings you to the search page. The Trademark Office preselects certain settings such as "Plural and Singular" and "Live and Dead," and you can just leave them alone. All you have to do is type in your term and click "Submit Query." As you can see, I typed in Jim H's term, "pink pelican." (Figure A.4)

Figure A.1. The Trademark Office Web site, *www.uspto.gov.*

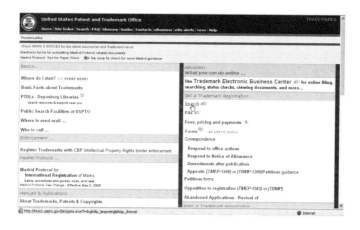

Figure A.2. The "Search" button.

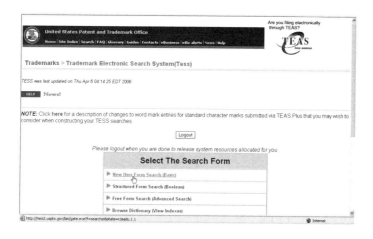

Figure A.3. The "New User Form" button.

Step 5. The trademark searches are very quick, and in no time at all up popped the results. In this case there was only one "hit." (Figure A.5) The bad news is that it is for the identical term! Oh no, Jim H is dead meat, right? Wrong! Remember, you can have the identical mark registered for different things, so long as there is no likelihood of confusion. So even though

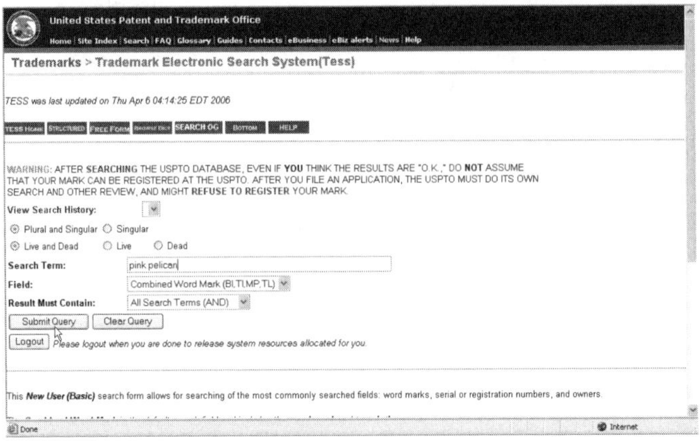

Figure A.4.   The search page.

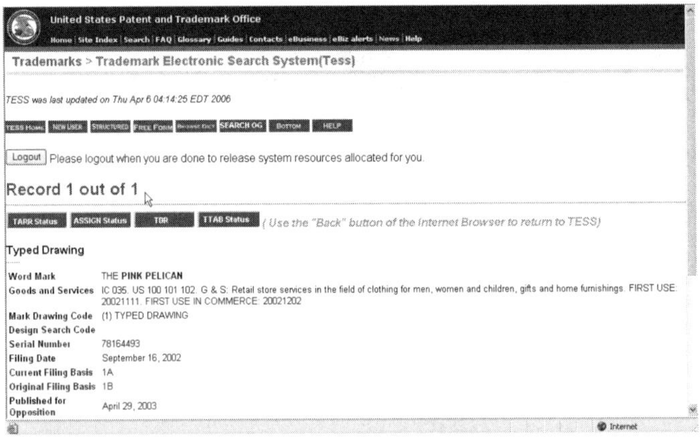

Figure A.5.   One listing was found.

the identical mark is already in the system, you must look at what the mark is being used for. In this case, the PINK PELICAN mark is being used for retail store services for clothing, gifts, and home furnishings. In my opinion, there is no likelihood of confusion in people's minds between a retail store and a flying hair dryer. But that's just my opinion! (See Chapter 2 if you have questions!)

Great Marks Keep Your Searches Simple

The PINK PELICAN mark qualifies under Shaffer's strategy as a "great mark." One of the benefits of a great mark is that it is not likely to have been used before by everyone else on the planet. If you choose to go with a suggestive, descriptive, or well-worn term, stand by! Look at the number of hits you get if you search the term "Sterling." (Figure A.6) This is a very serious-sounding mark, not silly at all like that Pelican thingy. Well, I hope you have serious fun analyzing the more than 1,000 hits that come up when you search it! Get my point? I hope so by now!

No matter what mark you choose, you can do a preliminary search of the actual trademark records at the Trademark Office, and it's free! Even if you aren't really sure if the results are good or bad, again, when and if you decide to file for registration, you can take them to your intellectual property attorney and let her or him tell you what it all means!

State Trademark Searches

Remember, unlike patents and copyrights, you can get a trademark registration in the state in which you do business. If you are going to have only one store in one state, then a state trademark is just the thing!

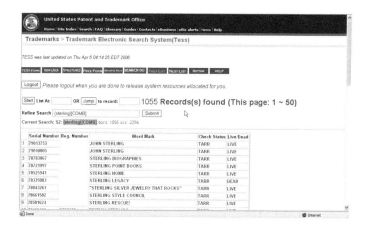

Figure A.6. The term "Sterling" lists several hits.

You can register trademarks in all 50 states. You can also search state trademarks online. Each state has its own process for registering trademarks. You can find your state's on-line process by consulting the Internet addresses listed below. If that doesn't work, you can do a simple Google search for "California trademark," for example, and that will lead you to the government site for California state trademarks as shown (Figure A.7). All states have similar processes, and the following example shows how a trademark search works in one.

A Sample State Trademark Search for PINK PELICAN

Here's how it works in Florida:

> *Step 1.* Go to the Florida Department of State Web site at *www.dos.state.fl.us* and click "Corporations." This is usually where states put the trademark division, but it may be somewhere different in your state. (Figure A.8)

> *Step 2.* This brings you to the Divisions of Corporations page, where you click "Corporate Information & On-Line Filing." (Figure A.9)

> *Step 3.* This brings you to a page with "Online Searches & Document Images," and you click that. (Figure A.10)

Figure A.7.   Government site for California state trademarks.

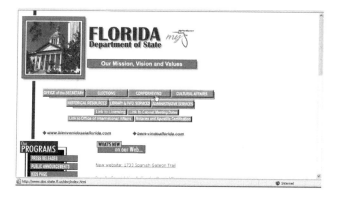

Figure A.8. Florida Department of State Web site.

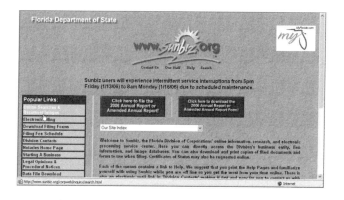

Figure A.9. Divisions of Corporations page.

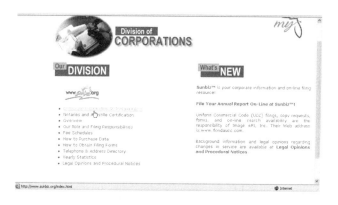

Figure A.10. Online Searches & Document Images page.

Step 4. Finally, you come to something that says "Trademarks," and you click that. (Figure A.11)

Step 5. This brings you to a state of exhaustion (sorry!). This also brings you to a screen with "Trademark Name List," and you click on it. (Figure A.12)

Step 6. At last you have reached the place where you can type in the mark you are thinking of registering, and you hit "Submit." (Figure A.13)

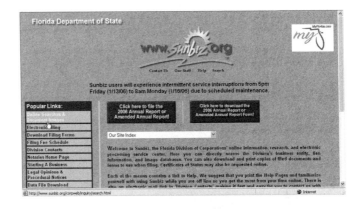

Figure A.11.   Trademarks button.

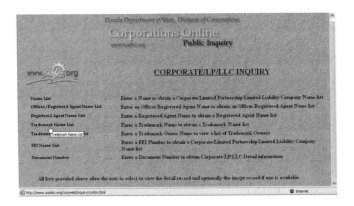

Figure A.12.   Trademark Name List button.

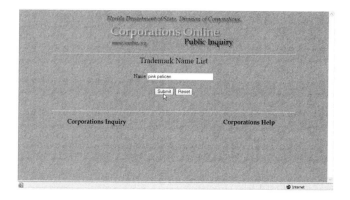

Figure A.13. Submit button.

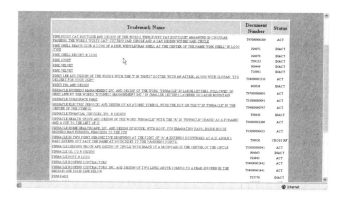

Figure A.14. Search for PINK PELICAN.

Step 7. This reveals that no one has previously applied for the term PINK PELICAN or a similar mark in the context of a mechanical device. (Figure A.14) That is good news!

While the state trademark search is similar to the federal trademark search, you should know that federal trademarks that have been registered trump state trademarks that are filed later. So even if your state trademark search looks good, you should also look to see if a federal mark preempts any state rights you might get. If nothing else, you can take the results of the state trademark search to your intellectual property attorney and let him or her explain what it means! And again, best of all, these Internet searches are free!

Why Even Get a State Trademark Registration?

You might be asking why you would want a state trademark if the federal registration covers all 50 states. Good question! If you've read this far, my answer won't surprise you. It's all about leverage. If you anticipate conflict over the mark you choose, a federal and a state registration gives you a choice of two courts you can go to, federal or state! That can make a big difference in terms of time and cost and your likelihood of prevailing. These are really the types of things your lawyer should advise you about, but because the price of registering is low, I think more protection is better!

Fifty State Trademark Office Web Sites

Here are all the government Web sites that serve as the starting points for registering a trademark in the different states. Obviously, these things can and do change! What's the point of having bureaucrats if they can't justify their existence by messing with things in the name of progress? Anyway, this list should be a good starting point for you!

- Alabama: *www.sos.al.us*

- Alaska: *www.dced.state.ak.us*

- Arizona: *www.azos.gov*

- Arkansas: *www.sos.arkansas.gov*

- California: *www.ss.ca.gov*

- Colorado: *www.sos.state.co.us*

- Connecticut: *www.sots.ct.gov*

- Delaware: *www.sos.state.de.us*

- Florida: *www.sunbiz.org*

- Georgia: *www.sos.state.ga.us*

- Hawaii: *www.ehawaii.gov*

- Idaho: *www.idsos.state.id.us*

- Illinois: *www.sos.state.il.us*

- Indiana: *www.in.gov/sos/business/trademarks*

- Iowa: *www.sos.state.ia.us*

- Kansas: *www.kssos.org*

- Kentucky: *www.apps.sos.ky.gov*

- Louisiana: *www.sec.state.la.us*

- Maine: *www.maine.gov*

- Maryland: *www.sos.state.md.us*

- Massachusetts: *www.sec.state.ma.us*

- Michigan: *www.michigan.gov*

- Minnesota: *www.sos.state.mn.us*

- Mississippi: *www.sos.state.ms.us*

- Missouri: *www.sos.mo.gov*

- Montana: *www.sos.state.mt.us*

- Nebraska: *www.sos.state.ne.us*

- Nevada: *www.sos.state.nv.us*

- New Hampshire: *www.sos.nh.gov*

- New Jersey: *www.state.nj.us*

- New Mexico: *www.sos.state.nm.us*

- New York: *www.dos.state.ny.us*

- North Carolina: *www.secretary.state.nc.us*

- North Dakota: *www.nd.gov*

- Ohio: *www.sos.state.oh.us*

- Oklahoma: *www.sos.state.ok.us*

- Oregon: *www.sos.state.or.us*

- Pennsylvania: *www.dos.state.pa.us*

- Rhode Island: *www.corps.state.ri.us*

- South Carolina: *www.scsos.com*

- South Dakota: *www.sdsos.gov*

- Tennessee: *www.state.tn.us*

- Texas: *www.sos.state.tx.us*

- Utah: *www.trademark.utah.gov*

- Vermont: *www.sec.state.vt.us*

- Virginia: *www.scc.virginia.gov*

- Washington: *www.secstate.wa.gov*

- West Virginia: *www.wvsos.com*

- Wisconsin: *www.sos.state.wi.us*

- Wyoming: *www.soswy.state.wy.us*

Trademark Usage Guidelines

You now know more about what a trademark is and isn't than most senior advertising executives! The problem is that your staff or advertising company personnel do not know as much as you do! In order to keep things consistent, and consistency is the key to proper trademark use, many businesses create trademark "cheat sheets" or guides to help them remember the dos and don'ts of proper trademark usage. Here is one for use by Jim H's PINK PELICAN Company for your consideration!

Trademark Usage Guide

All trademarks must serve *first* to identify the particular goods or services with which they are used, and *second* to distinguish those goods or services from other, similar goods and services in the marketplace. The following general rules of trademark usage all have the goal of enabling our PINK PELICAN trademark to perform these necessary functions.

General Trademark Use Rules

1. Always use our PINK PELICAN mark in text as an adjective, not as a noun or verb.

    Examples:

    Correct: PINK PELICAN flying hair dryers get you there fast and dry!

    Correct: All truly sophisticated people buy NIKE tennis shoes.

    Incorrect: Go out and buy NIKES.

    Incorrect: Be sure to XEROX it when you need a high-quality photocopy.

2. Always use the generic name for the goods along with our trademark. For extra emphasis, insert the word "brand" between the mark and the generic name.

Examples:

Correct: Buy PINK PELICAN flying hair dryers.

Also *Correct*: Buy PINK PELICAN brand flying hair dryers.

3. Always use our PINK PELICAN mark consistently. Do not pluralize the mark by adding an "s" or form a false singular by dropping an "s" that is properly part of the mark. Do not use the mark in a possessive form. Do not change the spelling, combine or separate words, or insert or omit hyphens.

4. Always use the proper trademark notice with our PINK PELICAN mark.

Examples:

PINK PELICAN™ flying hair dryers (use the symbol ™ while our mark is not federally registered but we are using PINK PELICAN as a mark and claiming trademark rights).

PINK PELICAN℠ flying hair dryer repair services (use ℠ for service marks).

PINK PELICAN® flying hair dryers (use the symbol ® only after the mark is federally registered).

or

PINK PELICAN* flying hair dryers (with one of the following footnotes, once the mark is federally registered: *Registered in U.S. Patent and Trademark Office, *or* *Reg. U.S. Pat. & Tm. Off.).

5. Use a special printing treatment to set the mark off from the rest of the text with which it appears.

Example: Fly higher and drier with ***PINK PELICAN*** flying hair dryers!

Appendix B

Protecting Your Invention by Yourself

It's your invention. You're stuck with it! (Just kidding!) When you have a great idea, the first question always is, "Now what do I do?" The point of this book is to answer that question and others! Here are some sample forms for you to use to get started in protecting your great idea for free. There is nothing magic in them, but they serve the magical purpose of transforming your raw idea into a tangible something that just might grow up into something terrific!

A Sample Invention Disclosure Form

Here is the Invention Disclosure form I use with my clients. Again, there is nothing magic in it. The most important thing to do in order to start protecting your great idea is to answer these three basic questions: (1) What is the problem? (2) What have other people done to solve the problem? (3) What have you done to solve the problem? The most important part of the form is the witness section at the end of document before the "Notes" section.

Confidential Proprietary Information Invention Disclosure Form

All data should be given in black ink using a typewriter or pen.

Date _____ 2006

TITLE OF INVENTION:

_____

INVENTOR(S): *(List all persons who contributed to the new or novel aspect of the invention. Attach additional sheets if more than three (3) co-inventors.)*

1. NAME:

_____

POST OFFICE ADDRESS:

_____

CITIZENSHIP:

_____

2. NAME:

_____

POST OFFICE ADDRESS:

_____

CITIZENSHIP:

_____

3. NAME:

_____

POST OFFICE ADDRESS:

_____

CITIZENSHIP:

_____

4. SUBJECT AND NATURE OF INVENTION: *(Briefly describe problem faced and innovative solution.)*

5. CONCEPTION DATE:

6. FIRST DISCLOSURE TO OTHERS: WHERE, WHEN, AND TO WHOM, AND WHETHER IN CONFIDENCE OR NOT: *(Specify records relied on and the location of those records. If no records are available, please indicate.)*

7. FIRST PRACTICE OF INVENTION: (a) LABORATORY, (b) FACTORY; WHERE, WHEN, AND TO WHAT EXTENT: *(Specify records relied on; if only (a), please indicate.)*

8. HAS THIS INVENTION BEEN PRACTICED COMMERCIALLY? IF SO, WHERE, WHEN, AND TO WHAT EXTENT: *(Any income-generating use; see Note 5.)*

9. GIVE DATES AND DETAILS REGARDING SAMPLES, INFORMATION, OR PUBLICATIONS RELATING TO THIS INVENTION THAT HAVE BEEN OR WILL BE GIVEN TO PERSONS OUTSIDE: *(See Note 5.)*

10. IF THE INVENTION HAS NOT BEEN EXPERIMENTALLY OR COMMERCIALLY PRACTICED, WHEN IS SUCH USE EXPECTED TO BEGIN?

11. ADVANTAGES OVER PRIOR STRUCTURES OR METHODS:

12. PATENTS OR OTHER KNOWN PUBLICATIONS YOU THINK ARE PERTINENT TO THIS INVENTION SHOWING SIMILAR OR OTHER SOLUTIONS TO THE PROBLEMS(S) SOLVED BY THIS INVENTION: *(Attach copies or state location where copies may be found.)*

13. THERE IS/ARE ATTACHED HERETO DESCRIPTION(S) OF THE INVENTION IDENTIFIED AS FOLLOWS: *(See Notes 2, 3, and 4.)*

    (a) Report..

(b) Letter...

(c) Drawings or Sketch...

(d) Photocopy of Laboratory Notebook Pages...............................

14. ANY OTHER INFORMATION THAT MIGHT BE CONSIDERED PERTINENT:

15. PRACTICAL IMPORTANCE OF THIS INVENTION AND EXTENT OF PROBABLE USE:

Inventor(s):

(1) Date

(2) Date

(3) Date

Witnesses: After **first** having agreed to keep this information confidential, I have read and understand the above disclosure.

(1) Date

(2) Date

Notes

The following points are of importance in securing sound national and international patent protection; inventors should understand them as completely as possible:

1. GIVE MORE INFORMATION, NOT LESS. Give not only the dates asked for, but note any records or circumstances that tend to establish the dates (e.g., laboratory notebooks, meetings or convention dates, etc.).

2. RECORD CONCEPTION AND PREPARE CONFIDENTIAL DISCLOSURE AS SOON AS POSSIBLE. To avoid possible loss of rights, inventions should be described in writing as promptly as possible after conception, and the writing and any accompanying drawings should be

signed and dated by the inventor and explained to two (2) other persons (not an inventor), who should also sign and date the writing and drawings as a witness.

3. PROVIDE AS COMPLETE A DESCRIPTION AS POSSIBLE. The description must be accurate and, in order to provide for broad protection, should include both the preferred method(s) or embodiment(s) and the broadest operable scope of the invention. For example, if an invention is designed for one particular purpose but could be useful for others too, state not only the preferred use and design but also other uses and designs that still accomplish the purposes of the invention. Avoid use of in-house shorthand nomenclature or any undefined abbreviations.

4. ATTACH ORIGINALS IF POSSIBLE. The originals of all pertinent records, except laboratory notebook pages, should be forwarded wherever possible with this form. In all cases, please supply reproducible copies.

5. NONCONFIDENTIAL DISCLOSURE OF INVENTION BEFORE FILING PATENT AFFECTS INTERNATIONAL RIGHTS. Although filing in the United States within one (1) year of the commercial use or publication will not bar a U.S. patent, such use or publication prior to filing may bar foreign patent rights.

Sample Non-disclosure Agreement (NDA)

Remember, there are lots of Non-disclosure Agreements. Lots and lots! Here is one that is not too long and not too short! Use it as a guide and for reference, *but always have your attorney check your NDA over before using it!*

Non-Disclosure Agreement

("Discloser") and _____ ("Recipient"), in consideration of the mutual covenants and agreements herein contained, hereby agree as follows:

1. *Disclosure:* Discloser may disclose to Recipient certain ideas and material concerning an idea for a: _____ ; which

may be oral or in documentary form or other hard copy, software, or other form or medium, including without limitation drawings, data, processes, and techniques, and which Discloser wishes to be held in strict confidence ("Confidential Material").

2. *Limited Use of Confidential Material:* Recipient may use the Confidential Material only for: ("Objectives") and for no other purpose. Nothing herein gives Recipient any license or other rights in any patent, copyright, trade secret, know-how, or other intellectual property right of Discloser.

3. *Protection and Non-Disclosure of Confidential Material:*

    (a) Recipient shall not disclose any portion of the Confidential Material to any party except its employees who must have access in order to carry out the Objectives and who are bound by written contract with Recipient not to disclose the Confidential Material to any other party; and upon Discloser's request, Recipient shall provide the names and addresses of such employees.

    (b) Recipient shall not permit the obscuring or removal of any wording or marking on the Confidential Material.

    (c) Upon Discloser's request, Recipient shall promptly deliver to Discloser all Confidential Material, and shall retain no copy of any Confidential Material.

4. *Ownership of Intellectual Property:* All inventions, discoveries, improvements, patents, and other intellectual property which is conceived, developed, made or perfected by Recipient or their agents or employees in connection with, or resulting from, Recipient's use of the Confidential Material shall be the exclusive property of Discloser. Recipient hereby assigns all rights, if any, therein to Discloser and shall promptly execute such documents as Discloser may request to perfect all such rights to Discloser.

5. *Exceptions:* Recipient shall have no obligations of confidentiality or use with respect to any portion of the Confidential Material:

    (a) In the public domain other than by reason of Recipient's default hereunder;

(b) In Recipient's possession in documentary or other tangible form prior to the date of this Agreement; or

(c) Disclosed to Recipient by a third party which has the right to make such disclosure; provided, that Recipient shall give Discloser notice at least thirty (30) days prior to any disclosure or use under this Section 5. Such notice shall identify (1) that portion of the Confidential Material to be disclosed or used, (2) the subsection of this Section 5 under which Recipient claims the right to disclose or use and (3) the full name and address of all persons to whom Recipient proposes to make disclosure.

6. *Rights and Remedies:* Recipient acknowledges that:

(a) The Confidential Material and all intellectual property embodied by the Confidential Material is the exclusive property of Discloser, and that Discloser will provide the Confidential Material to Recipient only if the parties enter into this Agreement, and that this Agreement does not create or transfer to Recipient any right of ownership in the Confidential Material or any intellectual property embodied therein; and

(b) Recipient shall be liable for any action of an employee or agent of Recipient where such action by the employee or agent would represent a breach of this Agreement if taken directly by Recipient; and

(c) The provisions of this Agreement are reasonably necessary to protect the confidential nature of the Confidential Material, and that a breach of this Agreement by Recipient or its employee or agent would cause Discloser irreparable harm for which it has no adequate remedy at law.

7. *Notice:* Notice hereunder must be in writing and shall be effective when actually delivered to the respective party at its address set forth above.

8. *Governing Law, Venue:* This Agreement shall be governed by, and construed according to, the laws of the State of _____, U.S.A. Any action arising from this Agreement shall be brought in a court of competent jurisdiction in County, _____, and the parties submit to the jurisdiction of that court.

9. *Entire Agreement:* This Agreement constitutes the entire understanding of the parties with respect to the Confidential Material and supersedes all prior oral or written agreements or understandings of the parties

with respect to the Confidential Material. This Agreement shall not be amended except in writing duly executed by the parties.

IN WITNESS WHEREOF, the parties have caused this Non-Disclosure Agreement to be executed as of the _____ day of _____, _____.
RECIPIENT:

DISCLOSER:

[Name of Company]
By:
By:
[Name of Person Signing]
Title:
Title: Inventor/Proprietary Owner

No Patent Search Is Perfect, but at Least This One Is Free

As we have discussed, many of the U.S. applications that are pending examination at the Patent Office are confidential and may not be searched no matter how much money you have to spend on a search. As a result, no patent search can ever be considered a guarantee that your great idea is patentable. Nonetheless, a great tool for folks with a great idea and no money to burn on a search is the search available at the U.S. Patent Office for free! Even though it is not perfect, it can be a source of a lot of useful information. (It is said, for example, that the Germans got the plans for the V2 rocket from a patent search at the U.S. Patent Office!)

A Sample Patent Search

Let's say your great idea involves a pest-free pet bowl. (I actually got my client Mr. Vega a patent for this great idea! See if you can find it!)

Step 1. Go to the Patent section of the USPTO Web site at *www.uspto.gov* and click "Search." (Figure B.1)

Step 2. This brings you to the search page, where the first thing you do is click "Online Patent Searches." (Figure B.2)

Figure B.1. Patent section of the USPTO Web site.

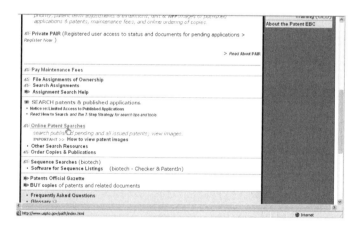

Figure B.2. Online Patent Searches button.

Step 3. This will bring you to the patent search page, where you should first click "How to Access and View Full-Page Images." (Figure B.3) That brings you to the page that explains what your system requirements must be for the viewer and lists free downloads you can choose from to enable you to view the patent drawings. (Figure B.4) You are really going to want to see the drawings to understand what the patent describes, so do

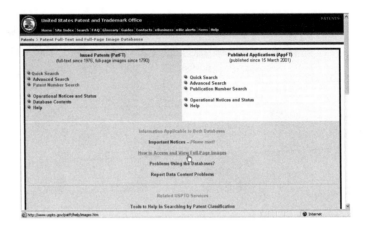

Figure B.3. How to Access and View Full-Page Images button.

Figure B.4. System requirements and free downloads.

this first! Then hit the "Back" button and at the search page, click "Quick Search." (Figure B.5) Once you log a hundred hours or so doing searches, you can probably move on to the "Advanced Search," but we are keeping it simple here!

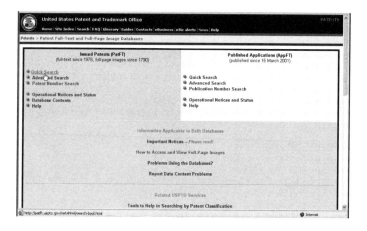

Figure B.5.   Quick Search button.

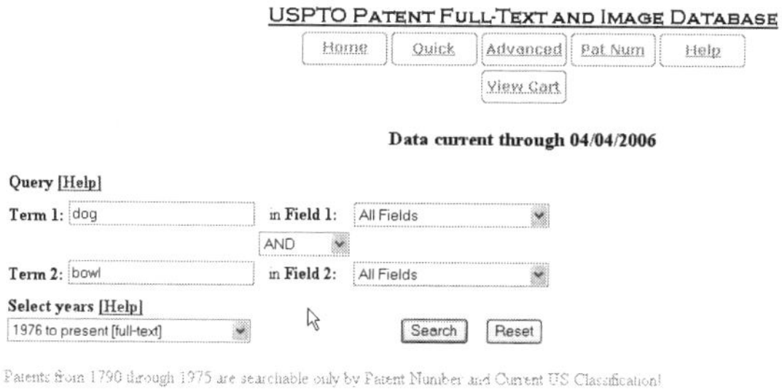

Figure B.6.   Choosing just the right words to search is the art in the science of doing a patent search.

Step 4. This brings up the search page itself, where you insert two descriptive words, one in "Term 1" and one in "Term 2." As you can see, I entered "dog" and "bowl." (Figure B.6) This is where the "art" of successful patent searching comes in. Choosing just the right words to search is the art in the science of doing a patent search. The better search words you use, the better search results you get!

You can see other options as in the block that says "All Fields" and "Select Years." My advice is to just leave them alone for now. These are the selections preset by the U.S. Patent Office and are a good place to start. Notice you are not searching every patent that has ever been issued from the Patent Office. They are working on it, but at this time this search works only for patents issued from 1976 on; earlier patents must be searched by patent number and U.S. Classification. Don't worry about it! You will have plenty to look at!

After inserting the two words, click "Search." (Figure B.7)

Step 5. It will take a few minutes for the results to turn up, so don't panic. You can see that 751 "patents" were returned for this search. (Figure B.8) Does that mean they are all related to dog bowls? No! It means the search engine found those two words somewhere in each of the listed patents! That is why the first patent on the list concerns a pet-repelling mat! Still, there are many relevant patents that are ready for you to read and review carefully, hour after hour after hour! Seven hundred and fifty-one, to be exact, on this search alone!

Step 6. At this point, you scroll down the list and see if any of the patents look relevant. Let's look at patent 48 on the first page of the list. Simply place your cursor on it and click away. (Figure B.9)

Step 7. This brings up the actual patent for the "Adjustable Height Pet Feeder," U.S. Patent number 6,854,419. Here is where you want to

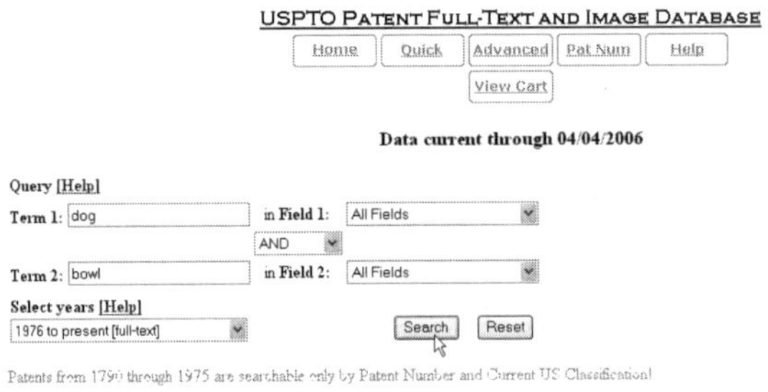

Figure B.7. The "Search" button.

USPTO PATENT FULL-TEXT AND IMAGE DATABASE

| Home | Quick | Advanced | Pat Num | Help |

| Next List | Bottom | View Cart |

Searching 1976 to present...

Results of Search in 1976 to present db for:
dog AND bowl: 751 patents
Hits 1 through 50 out of 751

[Next 50 Hits]

[Jump To] [_____]

[Refine Search] dog AND bowl

PAT NO. Title
1 7,021,244 T Pet repelling mat
2 7,018,945 T Composition and method for treating fibers and nonwoven substrates
3 7,017,518 T Device and method for reducing spillage in and around a dog bowl
4 7,016,828 T Text-to-scene conversion
5 7,011,826 T Control of acidosis

Figure B.8. Seven hundred and fifty-one "patents" were returned for this search.

27 6,916,469 T Gellable ant bait matrix
28 6,912,970 T Animal nourishment bowl
29 6,910,965 T Pari-mutuel sports wagering system
30 6,908,634 T Transglutaminase soy fish and meat products and analogs thereof
31 6,905,688 T Albumin fusion proteins
32 6,904,870 T Products and methods for improving animal dental hygiene
33 6,901,610 T High performance valve assembly for toilets
34 6,901,399 T System for processing textual inputs using natural language processing techniques
35 6,900,033 T Methods and compositions for modulating ACE-2 activity
36 6,899,666 T Blood processing systems and methods
37 6,897,291 T pH sensitive potassium channel in spermatocytes
38 6,890,748 T Production of lysosomal enzymes in plants by transient expression
39 6,890,549 T Compositions comprising dietary fat complexer and methods for their use
40 6,887,696 T Production of lysosomal enzymes in plants by transient expression
41 6,886,715 T Vending system for pet items and method
42 6,878,806 T Human secreted protein HTEEB42
43 6,875,595 T Nematode fatty acid desaturase-like sequences
44 6,866,863 T Ingestibles possessing intrinsic color change
45 6,862,465 T Device and method for determining analyte levels
46 6,857,391 T Animal toilet enclosure
47 6,855,542 T Chamber with adjustable volume for cell culture and organ assist
48 6,854,419 T Adjustable height pet feeder
49 6,846,968 T Production of lysosomal enzymes in plants by transient expression
50 6,846,506 T Food product

http://patft.uspto.gov/netacgi/nph-Parser?Sect1=PTO2&Sect2=HITOFF&p=1&u=/netahtml/search-bool.html&r=48f=G&l=50&col=AND&d=ptxt   Internet

Figure B.9. Look at patent 48 on the first page.

have the image-viewing software already downloaded so that you can look at the figures in the patent, the so-called patent drawings. Having done so, you click the "Images" button. (Figure B.10)

Step 8. That brings up an electronic copy of the actual patent! (Figure B.11) How cool is that! You can click on any part of the patent you

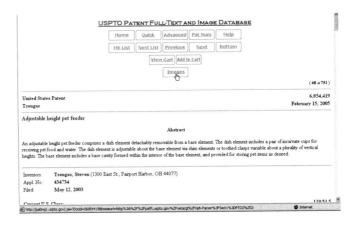

Figure B.10. The "Images" button.

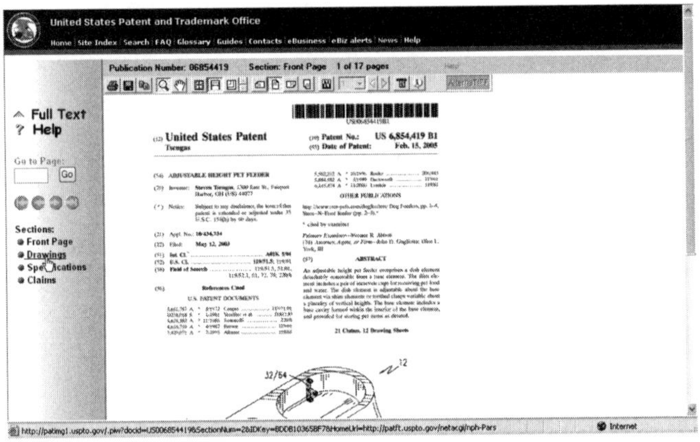

Figure B.11. The patent page.

wish to see first, or print it out if you wish. To get a quick sense of what the invention is about, I would first look at the drawings. (Figure B.12) Just hit the forward arrow to look at the next page of drawings.

Step 9. Because now you know how important the claims are, and that no matter what the figures show, what you get is covered in the claims section, I would look next at the claims by clicking on the "Claims"

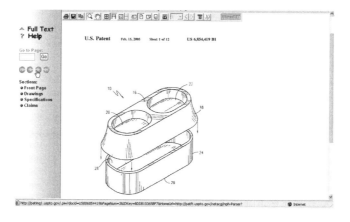

Figure B.12. Sample drawing of dog bowl.

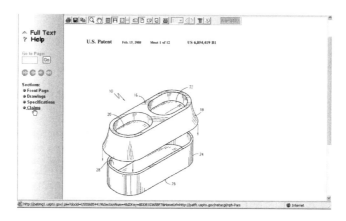

Figure B.13. The "Claims" section.

section. (Figure B.13) Again, as you know from Chapter 3, the claims define the limits of the patent for this and every other invention. This will bring up the section of the patent with those consecutively numbered paragraphs, starting with the broadest claim, claim one. (Figure B.14) The broader the claims are for your great idea, as we have discussed, the better! Knowing how to read claims will also give you an idea of how broad the other guy's protection is. (Review Chapter 3 if you have any questions!)

Figure B.14. Sample of claim one.

At a Minimum, the Pictures Should Help

Certainly, the more searches you do, the better you will be at it. Likewise, the more patents you read, the more sense they will make. Now, I am not suggesting that you give up your day job to become a professional patent searcher. Nor am I suggesting you even actually read all the patents you turn up. Even if you don't read them, the pictures can show you devices that look like they may be similar to yours, and if and when you ever decide to apply for a patent, you can take your search results and let your patent attorney tell you what it means! Best of all, it's free!

What If You Need a Patent Attorney?

You wouldn't be reading this book if you already knew how to protect your idea. You may realize after reading it that there are lots and lots of pitfalls for the unwary person with a great idea. So you may come to the conclusion that getting professional help is a good idea. But where do you find patent attorneys? You can't swing a bat without hitting a personal injury attorney, it seems. (This would be bad, of course, because they sue people for hitting other people with bats for a living!) But where are all the patent attorneys? Well, there aren't that many of them, actually. As of March 2006 there were 24,622 active patent attorneys and 7,563 active patent agents. A patent attorney is a person with a technical degree that has passed the patent bar exam and some state bar exam. A patent agent is a person with a technical degree that has passed the patent bar and can help you patent your great idea, but this person is not an attorney-at-law and cannot handle contracts, licenses, trademarks, or any other "practice of law." Remember, once you find a patent attorney, you have most likely found an intellectual property lawyer too who can help you protect your great idea in multiple other ways in addition to a patent!

Six Ways to Skin a Cat (Find a Patent Attorney)

Here are my thoughts on how to find a patent attorney, starting with the best way, in my opinion. Remember this, though: Even if you do not happen to have a patent attorney in your town, patent attorneys are licensed by the federal government and can practice anywhere in the United States! I have never even been to Idaho, and I have a patent client there!

1. Ask a lawyer you know and trust.

Most people know a lawyer. There are lots of lawyers, after all! So an easy way to find a patent attorney is to ask a lawyer you know and trust for the name of the patent attorney he or she uses. This does not mean that you take his or her word over your own personal interview and evaluation of the patent attorney, but at least it will get you to one in a hurry!

2. Ask the Small Business Development Center.

Most communities have a Small Business Development Center (SBDC) that is focused on helping small businesses. As you can imagine, the question of how to protect an idea comes up often at the SBDC. Ask them for a referral!

3. Ask the Chamber of Commerce.

Same deal as with the SBDC. Business is the business of chambers of commerce, and they often have a referral network that includes patent attorneys!

4. Look one up in Martindale-Hubbell.

Martindale-Hubbell is a well-known legal directory. They have a Web site, *www.martindale.com*, where you can search for lawyers by type of law, location, and name, among other things! It is pretty impersonal, but at least it gets you a name and a number. Martindale-Hubbell also lists peer-awarded ratings for law firms and lawyers. The highest rating is an AV rating.

5. Do a Google search.

Why not? You can search just "patent attorneys," which will bring up the U.S. Patent Office Web site and thousands of other listings, or you can search "patent attorneys+Georgia" and get a more focused result. Obviously, there are lots of other ways to search and words to use. The Internet is incredible, but sometimes it just has too much information!

6. Go to the U.S. Patent Office Web site.

Last on the list and first in my heart is the United States Patent and Trademark Office Web site. Go to it and click "Registered Patent Attorneys and Agents." (Figure B.15) This brings you to the search site where you can search "Listing by Geographic Region," (Figure B.16) which includes all 50 states plus the territories and possessions of the United States! It's worth a shot, and they have pretty accurate records as to who is and who is not a registered patent attorney!

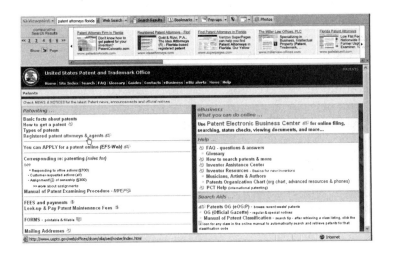

Figure B.15. Registered Patent Attorneys and Agents page.

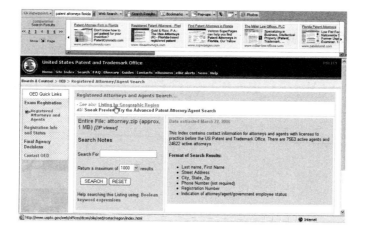

Figure B.16. Listing by Geographic Region page.

Appendix C

Doing Your Own Copyright Application

Fewer and fewer clients are asking me to prepare and file copyright applications for their original works of art and authorship. Some, with heavy output and sufficient budgets, do, but many people take my advice and try to file their copyright applications themselves.

Where to Start?

The application forms are available online at *www.copyright.gov*. (Figure C.1) Just about every piece of information you might ever want to know about copyrights is available at this user-friendly site. Typically, if you have done an original ad, it is a "Literary Work" and you would click on that button. (Figure C.2) This takes you to the page for form TX (for "textual" material). (Figure C.3) If you click on that, a PDF will be opened for the four-page form that you can fill out on your computer or print and fill out by hand! (Figure C.4)

As you can see, the form comes with instructions and is very user friendly! If nothing else, you can give it a go filling out the form and then take it to your attorney to review for accuracy. I think this is a good strategy if it is your first time filling out the form. Then, when you create another original work of authorship, you can use the first one as a guide!

Figure C.1. Copyrights Web site.

Figure C.2. Literary Work button.

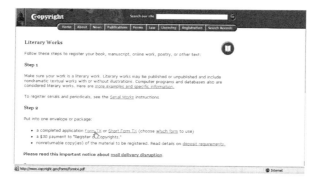

Figure C.3. Form TX button.

Figure C.4. Form TX.

Example of How to Fill Out a Form

Original works of art use form VA (for "Visual Arts"). Again, all the various forms for the various types of copyrightable material are available at this site! And…it's free! Here is an example of what a completed form VA would look like for the original artwork that Design Company Inc. created for Pink Pelican Inc. for the PINK PELICAN brand.

After you click on the form VA, you first have to enlarge the image by clicking on the "+" button. (Figure C.5) Then you scroll to page 1 of the application. Then you can fill in the form online! How cool is that! Read the instructions and fill in the first four blocks on the front page. Block 1 is the title.

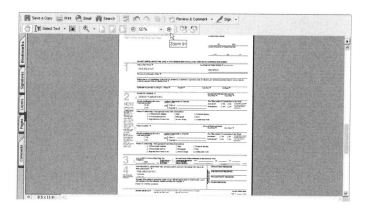

Figure C.5. Page 1 of form VA.

Because we are filing to protect the drawing of the Pink Pelican that will be used as the brand logo, Jim H has decided to call the title of this work of art Pink Pelican. Pretty easy so far, right?

In block 2 you insert the name of the design or graphics company you hired to do the drawing. Remember, you must have a written transfer of ownership of the copyright to own it even if you pay for it! Anyway, Jim H has typed in the design company name and checked the little block below it saying that the work done by Design Company Inc. was a work for hire created within that company. That is why Design Company Inc. is listed as the "Author."

In block 3 you fill in the date of creation or publication. In this case, the drawing has not been published yet, so the year of creation is all that is required.

Block 4 is the most important block on the form. It is a listing of who is claiming the copyright! Here Jim H proudly lists himself as the copyright claimant by indicating in the "Transfer" section of block 4 that he is the owner of the copyright by "Written Contract." This refers to the written agreement between Jim H and Design Company Inc. that says, "Jim H paid for the artwork of the Pink Pelican, we created it, and we hereby transfer all right, title and interest including copyright in the Pink Pelican art work to Jim H" or words to that effect!

Page 2 begins with block 5, and the answer is "No" previous registrations. (Figure C.6) If Jim H modifies the drawing to include a multicolored image, he would reference it as an "earlier registration." Nothing else needs to be filed in until block 7b, where Jim H enters his address for receiving correspondence,

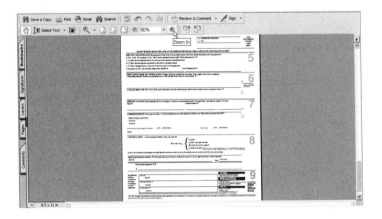

Figure C.6. Page 2 of form VA.

and the same information is put in block 9. In block 8 he certifies that he is the "owner of the exclusive rights," and that's it for filling out the form.

Note that the form must be submitted as a two-sided document, not as two separate pages. And, most importantly, Jim H must send in the completed and signed form, $30, and the deposit material, which in this case, because it is an unpublished work, consists of one copy of the drawing of the Pink Pelican! The process will take several months, but the date of the application will be the start date of the registration that follows. They will even communicate by e-mail with you if they have any questions about what you submitted!

If the Work Is Original, Forget About a Copyright Search

While it makes sense to search patents and trademarks, so far as original works of art and authorship are concerned, it makes *no sense* to search to see if what you have done has been done before! In fact, if you had never seen or heard of the book *Gone With the Wind* and happened to write the same book line for line, word for word, exactly, *both* works would be protectable as "original" works of authorship. In the real world, this does not happen. As a result, so long as you make sure that every ad, song, or piece of software you create is original, skip the search! There is a place to search copyright records, however, if you have a need to. (Figure C.7) And if you click the "Search Records" tab, you will be taken to a place to start a variety of searches of registered copyrighted materials. (Figure C.8)

And now, good luck, so long, and thanks for all the fish! The End! Of this, anyway!

Figure C.7.   Copyright searches.

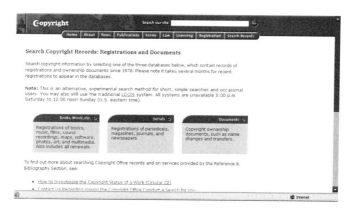

Figure C.8.   Start copyright searches here.

Index

Reader Feedback Sheet

Your comments and suggestions are very important in shaping future publications. Please e-mail us at *moreinfo@maxpress.com* or photocopy this page, jot down your thoughts, and fax it to (850) 934-9981 or mail it to:

Maximum Press
Attn: Jim Hoskins
605 Silverthorn Road
Gulf Breeze, FL 32561

IBM Software for e-business on demand
by Douglas Spencer
384 pages
$49.95
ISBN: 1-931644-17-9

Building an On Demand Computing Environment with IBM
by Jim Hoskins
152 pages
$39.95
ISBN: 1-931644-11-X

IBM On Demand Technology for the Growing Business
by Jim Hoskins
96 pages
$29.95
ISBN: 1-931644-32-2

Exploring IBM Server & Storage Technology, Sixth Edition
by Jim Hoskins
288 pages
$54.95
ISBN: 1-885068-28-4

Building on Your OS/400 Investment
by Jim Hoskins
120 pages
$29.95
ISBN: 1-931644-09-8

Building on Your AIX Investment
by Jim Hoskins
104 pages
$29.95
ISBN: 1-931644-08-X

Conquering Information Chaos in the Growing Business
by Jim Hoskins
68 pages
$29.95
ISBN: 1-931644-33-0

Exploring IBM @server pSeries, Twelfth Edition
by Jim Hoskins
and Robert Bluethman
352 pages
$54.95
ISBN: 1-931644-04-7

To purchase a Maximum Press book, visit your local bookstore
or call 1-800-989-6733 (US/Canada) or 1-850-934-4583 (International)
online ordering available at *www.maxpress.com*

Exploring IBM @server zSeries and S/390 Servers, Eighth Edition
by Jim Hoskins and Bob Frank
464 pages
$59.95
ISBN: 1-885068-91-3

Exploring IBM @server xSeries, Twelfth Edition
by Jim Hoskins, Bill Wilson, and Ray Winkel
208 pages
$49.95
ISBN: 1-885068-83-2

Marketing with E-mail, Third Edition
by Shannon Kinnard
352 pages
$29.95
ISBN: 1-885068-68-9

Marketing on the Internet, Seventh Edition
by Susan Sweeney, C.A., Andy MacLellen & Ed Dorey
216 pages
$34.95
ISBN: 1-931644-37-3

Protect Your Great Ideas for Free!
by Nevin Shaffer
184 pages
$29.95
ISBN: 1-931644-47-0

101 Ways to Promote Your Web Site, Sixth Edition
by Susan Sweeney, C.A.
432 pages
$29.95
ISBN: 1-931644-46-2

101 Internet Businesses You Can Start From Home Second Edition
by Susan Sweeney, C.A.
432 pages
$29.95
ISBN: 1-931644-48-9

Internet Marketing for Less Than $500/Year, Second Edition
by Marcia Yudkin
352 pages
$29.95
ISBN: 1-885068-69-7

To purchase a Maximum Press book, visit your local bookstore
or call 1-800-989-6733 (US/Canada) or 1-850-934-4583 (International)
online ordering available at *www.maxpress.com*